ASK
HIM
FOR
COURAGE
WITH
CANCER

Jane Trufant Harvey

E**v**ergreen
PRESS

Mobile, Alabama

Ask Him for Courage With Cancer
by Jane Harvey
Copyright ©2012 Jane Harvey

Author photo by:
Heidi Bower

ISBN 978-1-58169-385-0
For Worldwide Distribution
Printed in the U.S.A.

Evergreen Press
P.O. Box 191540 • Mobile, AL 36619
800-367-8203

DEDICATION

Joyce Bassemier Trufant
Charles Reynes Trufant
It was a privilege to be your daughter.

IN HONOR OF

Angelle Albright • Joan Altemuehle
Sandra Bisgaard • Townsend Bessent
Milissa Block • Susan Bopp • Marguerite Celestin
Alexandra Dedinsky • Bridget Eichhold • Gaylynn Falgoust
Nancy Fratzke • Jane Gorman • Marti Gorman • Toni Henry
Debbie Kamenar • Lisa Kavanaugh • Matthew Kelly
Trey Kertz • Alexis Landry • Aimee Melancon
Carolyn Briwa O'Rear • Fr. Ron Reider
Renee Silva • Tom Williams

IN MEMORY OF

Lou Babin • Christian Barker • Carl Barré
Aline Blanchard • John Blanchard
Odette Blanchard • Spencer Boyer
Elizabeth Dunford • Tommy Gorman
Pheeny Holt • Turner Holt • Katie Cantrelle
George "Tommy" Melancon
Dean McCloskey • Mary Lou O'Neill • Vicki Saterlee
Charles Reynes Trufant • Geri Soileau Trufant
Joyce Bassemier Trufant
Mary Trufant Roark • Fr. Alan Weseman

ACKNOWLEDGMENTS

So many people are responsible for helping and encouraging me to make *Ask Him for Courage With Cancer* a reality.

To all the people who *fight* cancer,

YOU ARE MY HEROES!

The Barré Family, the Boyer Family, the Barker Family, the Dunford Family; losing a child is every parent's nightmare. Each of these families has kept a written journal of their cancer experiences and allowed me the honor and privilege of peering inside their personal world of love, faith, courage, hope, strength, determination, vulnerability, heartbreak, and unspeakable grief. Angel Carl, Angel Spencer, Angel Christian, and Angel Elizabeth—you and your families continue to profoundly impact my life.

To my incredibly adorable, amazing husband and love of my life, Bobby, enough said!

To Angelle Albright, Joan Altemuehle, Greg and Jackie Barré, Milissa Block, Lauren Harvey Cothran, Nancy Fratzke, Tracy Gammon, Taylor Harvey, Elizabeth Harvey Icamina, Diane Yohana Kelly, Mary O'Neill, Charlene Shelton, Anne Trufant, Mary Trufant, and Sally Trufant for reading through the many, many drafts of this book and for putting up with my maniac self and all the changes I kept making. I just wanted so desperately to get it right.

To my family, I treasure you! I am the luckiest girl in the world to have you.

Finally, to my publisher, Evergreen Press,

Thank you again, for believing in me.

CONTENTS

INTRODUCTION

Cancer altered my life. It came uninvited and stole things from me, irreplaceable things. One day everything was fine and the next...not even close! I kept trying to figure out how to turn everything that is upside down and inside out, back to normal.

What I had to learn and accept was that I had a "new normal." But I still felt helpless and out of control.

Ask Him for Courage With Cancer was written so that you will know with absolute certainty that cancer *does not* have all the power. That you *are not* helpless. That God is your strength in this fight. That He will protect you and help you stand against all that cancer relentlessly tries to steal. In the process, He will teach and guide your heart....and if you let Him, He will help you discover life-changing things about yourself and those you love.

He never promises life will be easy, only that He will never leave your side.

I remember my mom telling me, "Janie, promise me you will remember one thing—loving and being loved is the *most important* thing in life; there is *nothing* more important. Promise me you will remember that."

I have remembered, Mom; your words are etched in my heart, and I ask God every day to help me live my life in that truth.
—Jane Harvey

I DON'T WANT YOU TO HAVE THIS BOOK!

Because if you have this book, you or someone you know has cancer.

I hate cancer! But I will tell you that it is a whole lot easier to have cancer *with* God than without Him.

Right now you are in the middle of a reality you don't want, wouldn't wish on your worst enemy, and yet for some reason are forced to bear, but you *will* bear it! God is going to give you the courage you will need to do it.

He will give you the kind of courage you didn't think you had. It's a courage that will even surprise you when you're in the midst of it. It's a moment in time when you suddenly realize that you have resources inside yourself that you knew nothing about. It's a moment in time when you feel totally helpless yet possess a courage and strength that seems to emerge from a deep place within you.

THE COURAGE TO RISE UP, DESPITE THE ODDS!

It is a divine courage that is given at a time when you are at your human weakest and God is at His most powerful. It is a gift; the gift of courage through the grace of God.

I want this book to encourage you and comfort you, but most importantly, I want this book to reveal that it's not about asking God to help you through this cancer experience; it's about asking God to help you through *this life*!

When you ask God to mold you and bring your desires into alignment with His, you are asking the character and power of God to begin the transforming work in and through you.

And I will be rejoicing for you!

There are 52 *Ask Him* theme pages. Each of them has corresponding scripture verses already written out so you don't have to go look them up.

Following the scripture page there are two additional pages that contain personal journal questions.

This book is designed for you to contemplate and pray about ONE *Ask Him* thought each WEEK, not each day! Repetitively reflecting on one thought for a week allows you to really embrace it and let it change you from the inside out.

PERSONAL JOURNAL

I'm going to make the instructions for your personal journal very, very easy. They are as follows: There are no instructions.

Now how's that for easy? If I might, though, I'd like to make a few suggestions and give you my thoughts as to why I wanted you to have this personal journal in the first place.

Cancer and serious illnesses are frightening. This book was written to help you find validation, encouragement, confidence, wisdom, hope, peace, and of course *courage* as you deal with and manage the changes your diagnosis has brought into your life. I wrote the book because I want you to understand how incredibly powerful it is to invite God into your cancer or serious illness. I wrote the book because I want you to know the enormous difference it makes to your emotional well-being when you rest and rely on someone greater than yourself.

So why not just read the book? Because reading and acknowledging something is not the same as being able to identify how the words affect you in a personal way.

Writing is about releasing. It's about bringing out what is stuck inside. It's about self-discovery. It peels back the layers of complex things and enables you to really process what is going on with you. It helps bring forth reasoning.

Releasing through writing is about taking a step further in the healing process. It helps you take ownership of your truth. And if you stand firm in your truth, you frequently uncover hidden thoughts and feelings that, if left unresolved, could potentially obstruct your path to healing.

This journal is designed to help you start conversations with God. It's about helping you understand that sometimes His greatest gifts are concealed in His greatest challenges for you.

This is not a journal that you will complete. It is an ongoing conversation you will begin sharing with God. Try to jot down the date of each entry so you'll always be able to go back and reflect on how far you've come or if you need to readdress certain issues that are keeping you anxious and frazzled.

When you *Ask Him* to help you, sit quietly and let Him speak to your heart, then write down what you think He would say as if He were sitting right beside you.

What's that, you say? You wouldn't know what to write? You've never spoken to God? God has never spoken to you?

Oooh, yes He has! At the top of some of the pages, there is a crown symbol. Underneath that symbol are words from scripture (the Bible). Those words are God speaking to you. They are important to know.

You can start by writing what you think God might want you to understand. Tell Him how you think and feel about the two scripture passages. And remember, there is no right or wrong way to journal. Do what feels most comfortable to you. You don't have to follow any guidelines, just write whatever you're thinking about that particular day or moment in time.

Just before I leave you to your journal writing, let me first remind you that the God you are writing and conversing with has only one, single, solitary, unchanging, intensely uncompromising attitude toward you—*He loves you*. He loved you yesterday, He loves you today, and He will love you tomorrow. He loves you more than every single thing He has ever created. He loves you more brilliantly than the sun, more infinitely than the stars. He loves you more than you can imagine or fathom. He loves the way you were, the way you are, and the way you will be. He loves all of you—the good parts, the bad parts, the strong parts, and the weak parts. He loves the whole package.

So my hope, as you begin your personal journal, is that every day you tell yourself over and over and over again that your God will always, always unceasingly love you more.

"For I know the plans I have for you," declares the Lord, "plans to prosper you and not to harm you, plans to give you hope and a future. Then you will call on me and come and pray to me, and I will listen to you. You will seek me and find me when you seek me with all your heart" (Jeremiah 29:11-13 NIV).

ASK HIM

...to help you quiet the chaos of cancer by holding you in the refuge of His peace.

One thing cancer is famous for is bringing a sense of bewilderment and dread.

Well, God is famous for a few things as well! One of those things is that in the midst of the chaos He can offer a sweet stillness, an inner tranquility to all who take refuge in Him.

He will shield and protect you in His perfect peace. He wants you to cast all your cares on Him. That means He wants *it all*—your distress, your anxiety, your chaos, and anything else that is burdening you. Releasing those things to Him enables you to receive the peace He wants to release in you.

When you need to quiet your mind and gain some perspective, when you need to quiet the chaos of cancer, all you need to do is run to Him.

He's ready to embrace you into the refuge of His peace because He *is* peace.

JOHN 14:27

Peace I leave with you; My [own] peace I now give and bequeath to you. Not as the world gives do I give to you. Do not let your hearts be troubled, neither let them be afraid. [Stop allowing yourselves to be agitated and disturbed; and do not permit yourselves to be fearful and intimidated and cowardly and unsettled.] (AMP)

1 PETER 5:7

Casting the whole of your care [all your anxieties, all your worries, all your concerns, once and for all] on Him, for He cares for you affectionately and cares about you watchfully. (AMP)

Journal

Envision yourself walking over to God, who stands anxiously waiting to take your burdens. He wants to relieve the heaviness in your heart so you can know His tranquility and peace.

In a quiet place, write down all the chaos that is overwhelming you right now. Invite Him into the chaos; *Ask Him* to give you His divine and all-encompassing sense of peace.

_____

_____

_____

_____

_____

_____

_____

_____

_____

_____

_____

_____

_____

The world looks at peace as something you have when everything is going your way. God's divine peace can be felt even in the midst of great tribulation.

Where does your peace come from; what are the specific people, places, or things that help you feel peaceful?

_____

_____

_____

_____

_____

_____

_____

_____

_____

_____

_____

_____

_____

_____

_____

_____

ASK HIM

...to remind you that it was no fluke, just His infinite wisdom, that "do not be afraid" is the most frequently repeated phrase in the Bible.

I know you are scared. I don't like those up-close and personal encounters with fear either, and I certainly don't like the paralyzing component that fear sometimes inflicts.

God knew that fear was going to be a huge issue for us. I know this to be true because He made a point of saying, "Do not be afraid" more than any other phrase in the Bible! That's pretty powerful. Since He doesn't want our lives to be controlled by fear and since you can't magically wish fear away, the only way to diminish its power is to identify and name what you fear, face it head-on, and give God the chance to help you courageously wrestle your way through it.

Fear is not the absence of courage. Fear is a hint reminding you that on the other side of fear is triumph. Each time you triumph over fear, transforming wisdom is there to take its place.

PSALM 27:1,3,5

The Lord is my Light and my Salvation—whom shall I fear or dread? The Lord is the Refuge and Stronghold of my life—of whom shall I be afraid? Though a host encamp against me, my heart shall not fear; though war arise against me, [even then] in this will I be confident. For in the day of trouble He will hide me in His shelter; in the secret place of His tent will He hide me; He will set me high upon a rock. (AMP)

ISAIAH 41:13

For I am the Lord, your God, who takes hold of your right hand and says to you, Do not fear; I will help you. (NIV)

Journal

Even though God doesn't want our lives to be controlled by fear, we sometimes find ourselves caught, stuck, and immobilized by it.

How do you react to fear?

What wisdom have you ever gained when you were able to wrestle your way through and triumph over fear?

Write a small prayer thanking God for making "do not be afraid" a prevailing theme throughout the Bible.

_____

_____

_____

_____

_____

_____

_____

_____

_____

_____

_____

_____

_____

Fear is a powerful force.

Do you have recurring fears that constantly jolt you with feelings of terror? Go back and reread pages 6 and 7. How can God help you face and triumph over fear? Write down how you think He could help you.

What are the reasons God gives you not to be afraid?

_____

_____

_____

_____

_____

_____

_____

_____

_____

_____

_____

_____

_____

_____

ASK HIM

...to help you keep in mind, when the Divine Physician is the head of your treatment team, anything is possible.

Okay, so you have a cancer diagnosis. For what it's worth, I think it stinks too. But it's time to get to work putting together the treatment team that's going to help you win this fight.

The most important feature of the treatment team is finding a leader who is both reliable and dependable.

Remember, the head of your treatment team works very closely with you and is involved in every decision...so you'll want the best.

And the best you shall have!

He's not in another country, He's not too busy to see new patients, He's got an incredible bedside manner, and He doesn't charge one cent for His expertise.

God's mission statement is clear, *"What is impossible with man is possible with God."*

So what are you waiting for...sign Him up!

LUKE 18:27

Jesus replied, "What is impossible with men is possible with God." (NIV)

PSALM 33:9

...because when he speaks, things happen. And if he says, "Stop!"—then it stops. (ERV)

Journal

One of the hardest things about cancer is having to make life-changing decisions about treatment options without being exactly qualified for it.

Your Divine Physician will keep a watchful eye over you. His voice leads to life, sound judgment, and peace, not oppression and confusion.

How can you include God in your decision-making process? Write out a brief prayer you can repeat to yourself before making a treatment decision.

_____

_____

_____

_____

_____

_____

_____

_____

_____

_____

_____

_____

What qualities do you think will be most important when choosing who will help you with your treatment and survivorship plan?

_____

_____

_____

_____

_____

_____

_____

_____

_____

_____

_____

_____

_____

_____

_____

_____

_____

ASK HIM

*...to assure you that it doesn't matter
if the only reason you came looking
for Him is because you have cancer;
it only matters to Him that you did.*

I have a friend named Angelle who was once what you might call a "wild one."

Then she was diagnosed with an aggressive form of breast cancer and told the probability that she would see her children graduate from high school was slim.

She knew about God, but He had never really fit very well into her lifestyle or schedule. Now she was in real trouble, and God was the only one she knew who did miracles.

So she prayed what she called her "foxhole" prayer: "Lord, I realize we don't know each other very well, but I have three small children and I'm scared."

When she confessed to her pastor that it was only because she was dying that she came looking for God, she will never, ever forget what he said. He said, "Angelle, God doesn't care *why* you've come; He's just ecstatic that you did. Welcome home!"

ISAIAH 54:10

"The mountains may disappear, and the hills may become dust, but my faithful love will never leave you. I will make peace with you, and it will never end." The Lord who loves you said this. (ERV)

2 CORINTHIANS 1:21-22

Now it is God who makes both us and you stand firm in Christ. He anointed us, set his seal of ownership on us, and put his Spirit in our hearts as a deposit, guaranteeing what is to come. (NIV)

Journal

One of the most incredible things about God is that He'll wait for you and welcome you anytime, anywhere, in any condition, no matter how long it takes.

The *only* thing that matters to Him is that you're here now.

Is it difficult for you to truly receive that unconditional acceptance? Why?

Has there been anyone else in your life from whom you felt such unconditional acceptance? Who is it? Is there someone in your life who needs the comfort of this same type of acceptance from you? Who is it?

_____

_____

_____

_____

_____

_____

_____

_____

_____

_____

_____

Do you know that God promises that His love will never leave you and that the peace He makes with you will never end? *Even* if there are times when you leave Him, He will *still* never stop loving you and giving you His peace. It's important during this time for you to know that God will take you exactly as you are, with all your faults and flaws.

Tell Him how it feels that He goes to such great lengths to reassure you about this.

_____

_____

_____

_____

_____

_____

_____

_____

_____

_____

_____

_____

ASK HIM

...to remind you to breathe in the power and strength of His peace and exhale the fear and anxiety that keeps you stressed.

Today I'm going to teach you a breathing technique I taught my Mom each time she felt overwhelmed by her cancer.

I'd say, "Mom, close your eyes and take a deep breath. Breathe in God's strength and peace. Now exhale your worries and anxiety. Breathe in His optimism, and breathe out your negativity. Breathe in His love, then breathe out your hostility."

After the first few breaths I could actually see a physical change in her body.

So, try it with me. Breathe in His confidence, then breathe out your doubt. Breathe in His protection, then breathe out your fear. Breathe in His acceptance, and breathe out your unworthiness. Breathe in His goodness, and breathe out your bitterness. Are you feeling better?

I'm so happy...breathe it in!

PSALM 29:11 AND PSALM 55:22

The Lord will give [unyielding and impenetrable] strength to His people; the Lord will bless His people with peace. (Psalm 29:11 AMP)

Cast your burden on the Lord [releasing the weight of it] and He will sustain you; He will never allow the [consistently] righteous to be moved (made to slip, fall, or fail). (Psalm 55:22 AMP)

PHILIPPIANS 4:6-7

Don't worry about anything, but pray and ask God for everything you need, always giving thanks for what you have. And because you belong to Christ Jesus, God's peace will stand guard over all your thoughts and feelings. His peace can do this far better than our human minds. (ERV)

Journal

The first part of this powerful breathing exercise is to focus and visualize the positive aspect of each word you breathe in. Then consciously receive for your body all the healing properties associated with it.

In the second part, the focus shifts to consciously exhaling and releasing each toxic word that interferes with healing.

Try and think of different word combinations you could integrate in these breathing exercises that might better suit the emotions and circumstances you face.

Now it's your turn. Fill in the blanks with the different word combinations that better suit the emotions and circumstances you face. (Revisit these pages often.)

Breathe in _____ Breathe out _____

Breathe in _____ Breathe out _____

Breathe in _____ Breathe out _____

Breathe in _____ Breathe out _____

_____

_____

_____

_____

_____

Write down what happens to your body physically, emotionally, and spiritually as you do this exercise.

_____

_____

_____

_____

_____

_____

_____

_____

_____

_____

_____

_____

_____

_____

_____

_____

_____

_____

_____

ASK HIM

...to revitalize your life with the healing energy of optimism.

Optimism is to believe with confidence in the power of good. It's a decision to entertain thoughts that will inspire and contribute to your peace of mind.

Optimists turn lemons into lemonade. They always see the glass half full rather than half empty. They handle difficulties by resolutely refusing to build or entertain imaginary obstacles that impede solutions.

When they come to a roadblock, they don't turn around feeling defeated; they regroup, rethink, and reframe each situation with the wholehearted belief that any dilemma imparts wisdom and that this wisdom then becomes the motivating force behind the development of another more prudent solution.

This kind of optimism refuels your body with inner health and healing energy. It elevates your mind to what is good and beautiful not only around you but beyond you. It gives you a tendency to expect the best. It looks for the best in others. It draws the very best to you and embraces the very best in you.

Take advantage of the powerful healing components in optimism. *Be revitalized!*

PROVERBS 4:23

Above all, be careful what you think because your thoughts control your life. (ERV)

PHILIPPIANS 4:8-9

For the rest, brethren, whatever is true, whatever is worthy of reverence and is honorable and seemly, whatever is just, whatever is pure, whatever is lovely and lovable, whatever is kind and winsome and gracious, if there is any virtue and excellence, if there is anything worthy of praise, think on and weigh and take account of these things [fix your minds on them]. Practice what you have learned and received and heard and seen in me, and model your way of living on it, and the God of peace (of untroubled, undisturbed well-being) will be with you. (AMP)

Journal

Elevate your mind, refuel your body, and revitalize your life by staying focused *only* on the good. Look, find, and receive the good!

If a negative thought comes, reject it immediately, and replace it with something positive.

Think back over everything that happened today. Make a list of the *good* things that happened. Perhaps it was a warm smile from another patient. Perhaps it was a parking spot close to the entrance or good news on some test results. Embrace and feel the healing energy.

_____

_____

_____

_____

_____

_____

_____

_____

_____

_____

_____

_____

Are some of your friends more optimistic than others? Who are the *really* optimistic ones? Write their names here. Think about calling them when you're having a hard time keeping your spirits up. Imagine how touched your friend would be if you called and said, "I'm calling because you're one of the most optimistic people I know, and I need some of that right now."

Go back and reread Philippians 4:8-9 on page 23. What things does it suggest you "fix your mind" on? How can those things help you stay optimistic?

_____

_____

_____

_____

_____

_____

_____

_____

_____

_____

_____

ASK HIM

...to remind you that it is impossible to be consumed by hopelessness with a mind empowered by God.

When you have God, you have everything that is most important. When your mind is empowered by God, you know that when your own human strength gives out, the power of His divine strength knows no bounds.

When you know God, you know that one of His most important messages is hope. Hope is a belief in and an expectation of something more that is yet to come.

Even in the most dire of circumstances, when your mind is empowered by God, you know that He wants more for you than you can ever imagine for yourself. You know that even though life is uncertain, His words direct, inspire, and motivate you not just to survive in this life but to thrive.

A mind empowered by God never loses hope because whatever is yet to come can only be whatever God's absolute *best* is for you. Be empowered to hope!

HEBREWS 6:18

These two things cannot change: God cannot lie when he says something, and he cannot lie when he makes an oath. So these two things are a great help to us who have come to God for safety. They encourage us to hold on to the hope that is ours. (ERV)

2 THESSALONIANS 2:16-17

We pray that the Lord Jesus Christ himself and God our Father will comfort you and strengthen you in every good thing you do and say. God loved us and gave us through his grace a wonderful hope and comfort that has no end. (ERV)

Journal

Hopelessness damages every defining feature of the human person.

What causes you to feel hopeless?

Using the scriptures on page 27, write down a little prayer you can say when you are feeling completely hopeless.

_____

_____

_____

_____

_____

_____

_____

_____

_____

_____

_____

_____

_____

_____

_____

_____

God's hope is empowering because His hope wants only your best.

What are some things you think God may have in store for you, that you can look forward to?

_____

_____

_____

_____

_____

_____

_____

_____

_____

_____

_____

_____

_____

_____

_____

_____

ASK HIM

...to remind you that your cancer is *not* some kind of punishment from God because of sin!

People who say that the root cause of sickness is sin are mistaken!

Just in case you aren't completely clear about what happened...over two thousand years ago someone willingly stepped forward and with great dignity and honor paid the price for *all* sin. All of it! Yours and mine! Sins past. Sins present, and even future sins we don't yet know we're going to commit.

That's why they call Him *Savior*. Before Jesus was in the picture, the wages of sin was death. So God made a way through His Son Jesus to bring restoration to the shattered relationships that sin kept destroying. Jesus would sacrifice his life by taking upon Himself the burden of the sins of the world—all of them!

This dramatic sacrifice by a Father of His Son speaks volumes on the depth and breadth of the merciful and loving heart of our God.

It is by the wounds of His son that we are healed and made whole.

We are infinitely forgivable, infinitely redeemable.

ISAIAH 53:5

But He was wounded for our transgressions, He was bruised for our guilt and iniquities; the chastisement [needful to obtain] peace and well-being for us was upon Him, and with the stripes [that wounded] Him we are healed and made whole. (AMP)

JOHN 9:2-3

And His disciples asked Him, "Rabbi, who sinned, this man or his parents, that he was born blind?" Jesus answered, "It was neither that this man sinned, nor his parents; but it was so that the works of God might be displayed in him." (NAB)

Journal

Did you know that God would have sacrificed His only Son to die on the cross even if it was to save *only you?*

You are worth it to Him!

One of God's best gifts is His mercy. You ask for forgiveness, and you are redeemed.

Who needs *your* mercy today?

_____

_____

_____

_____

_____

_____

_____

_____

_____

_____

_____

_____

_____

_____

You may not be perfect, but you are not sick because of it. When you look at the scripture on the previous page, John 9:2-3, do you think that it's possible that God might be made visible through you?

Be on the lookout for ways God may be using you to make Himself visible to someone else. Can you think of any recent examples?

_____

_____

_____

_____

_____

_____

_____

_____

_____

_____

_____

_____

_____

ASK HIM

...to please take away any apprehension that might keep you from graciously accepting the help and generosity of others.

It is natural, even with cancer, to keep pushing yourself to continue handling every detail of your life.

Losing the ability to take care of yourself or your family, even for brief periods of time, can be agonizing.

When our lives become unmanageable, why do we still hesitate when someone offers to help?

For most of us, to accept help represents weakness, losing a sense of independence, or not wanting to inconvenience anyone.

This is way bigger than that! This is about you stepping aside to give others an opportunity to give from their heart.

It's about you being receptive and humbly embracing their spirit of generosity. When you let others help you, your gift to them (yes! your gift to them) is *in the way* you graciously accept their gift to you!

HEBREWS 13:1-2

Continue loving each other as brothers and sisters in Christ. Always remember to help people by welcoming them into your home. Some people have done that and have helped angels without knowing it. (ERV)

COLOSSIANS 4:5-6

Conduct yourselves wisely toward outsiders, making the most of the opportunity. Let your speech always be with grace, as though seasoned with salt, so that you know how you should respond to each one. (NAB)

Journal

When your life has become unmanageable, why are you still bullheadedly hesitating when someone offers to help?

Write a list of words describing how it makes you feel when you have to ask for help.

If your best friend wrote this list and shared it with you, what would you say to reassure her or him?

What have you learned about yourself?

_____

_____

_____

_____

_____

_____

_____

_____

_____

_____

_____

_____

_____

_____

On page 34 it says that it's about *you* being receptive and humbly embracing another person's spirit of generosity.

When you let someone help you, your gift to them is in the way you graciously accept their gift to you!

Had you ever considered that the way in which you receive a gift could be a gift, in and of itself, to the giver?

I know this may seem silly, but when you have to do something you aren't necessarily comfortable with; it helps to think it through ahead of time. So, take a moment and write down what you are going to say when you graciously accept someone's offer of help. Practice saying it!

ASK HIM

...for the wisdom to realize that a positive attitude is the one thing you can *control when everything else seems out of control.*

There are many things in this life we cannot control. No time has this statement ever felt more real or had more of an impact than the day you were given a cancer diagnosis.

You're challenged on a daily basis to try and maintain some sense of sanity in what feels like an insane situation.

In the intricacies of the human brain, you have the miraculous ability to reason. This simply means you have the ability to adjust the way you will mentally respond to any given situation.

So even when everything around you seems totally out of control, there is something you *can* control—having a positive attitude.

Believe me when I tell you that this is not an easy or simple decision. What it is, however, is a *calculated* decision. It's also an immensely powerful decision that will enormously influence *everyone* and *everything* around you.

Attitude is a game changer. Take control.

PROVERBS 17:22

A joyful heart is the health of the body, but a depressed spirit dries up the bones. (NAB)

MATTHEW 12:35

The good man from his inner good treasure flings forth good things, and the evil man out of his inner evil store-house flings forth evil things. (AMP)

Journal

When everything around you seems out of control, appropriate choices and decisions are difficult at best.

In the space below, write out a prayer asking God to settle your spirit so you'll be in the best possible frame of mind to make the best possible choices.

_____

_____

_____

_____

_____

_____

_____

_____

_____

_____

_____

_____

_____

_____

_____

_____

Write a list of the things that you feel are most out of control right now.

How would approaching your list with a positive attitude change things?

How would it affect everyone and everything around you? Why?

_____

_____

_____

_____

_____

_____

_____

_____

_____

_____

_____

_____

_____

_____

ASK HIM

...to assure you when you're too overwhelmed to pray; He hears from your heart what your voice can't express.

I wish I could tell you that consistent prayer brings consistent peace. But unfortunately there are times when life gets out of hand, and you find yourself so preoccupied and distracted that time for quiet prayer seems impossible.

Ironically, it's in times like these that you most desperately want to feel the comfort of God, but how can you convey something to God when you're so overwhelmed you can't fully understand what's going on yourself?

I want to assure you of something very, very important. God hears from your heart what your voice can't express.

If for any reason you are not able to remember to pray or are too overwhelmed to pray, God sends His Spirit to intercede for you so you don't have to say or do anything.

In His incredible love and compassion, He will simply engage your heart so not a sound would need to pass your lips.

ROMANS 8:26-27

Also, the Spirit helps us. We are very weak, but the Spirit helps us with our weakness. We don't know how to pray as we should, but the Spirit himself speaks to God for us. He begs God for us, speaking to him with feelings too deep for words. God already knows our deepest thoughts. And he understands what the Spirit is saying, because the Spirit speaks for his people in the way that agrees with what God wants. (ERV)

PSALM 139:23

Search me, O God, and know my heart; test me and know my anxious thoughts. (NIV)

Journal

Have you ever really taken time to think about the mysteries of God?

Once you've come through a particularly trying time, close your eyes, take a deep breath and exhale slowly, now *thank Him* for having made provisions for the times you are too overwhelmed to think, much less pray.

Write your prayer of thanksgiving here.

_____

_____

_____

_____

_____

_____

_____

_____

_____

_____

_____

_____

God wants you to put into words what's overwhelming you. Read over what you've written.

If God wanted to write a little note to comfort and reassure you, write down what you think He would say.

_____

_____

_____

_____

_____

_____

_____

_____

_____

_____

_____

_____

_____

_____

_____

_____

ASK HIM

...to remind you that sustained courage thrives in the echoed words: God, I trust in You; God, I trust in You.

Trust is when you can *let go* with the sure knowledge that God's good is at work for you.

Trust is when you can be confident God's good is not only His divine plan but also His perfect and divine timing as well.

Courage is when you can trust both His plan and His timing even in the midst of uncertainty.

Scripture tells you—*lean on, trust in, and be confident in the Lord with all your heart and mind, and do not rely on your own insight or understanding.*

Things don't always make sense to us because God does things with a divine perspective. We, on the other hand, are much more interested in the "now" perspective.

God is what you need on this journey. He is your sustaining courage. He is power, wisdom, and goodness.

Embrace Him and live courageously! Trust!

2 SAMUEL 22:31

"As for God, his way is perfect; the word of the Lord is flawless. He is a shield for all who take refuge in him." (NIV)

1 THESSALONIANS 5:23-24

We pray that God himself, the God of peace, will make you pure—belonging only to him. We pray that your whole self—spirit, soul, and body—will be kept safe and be blameless when our Lord Jesus Christ comes. The one who chose you will do that for you. You can trust him. (ERV)

 Journal

Do you trust that God's good is at work in you? Have you had an experience where you trusted someone and they came through for you? How did you feel while you were waiting to find out? Think about how you felt once you knew they could be trusted. *That's* the feeling God wants you to have when you put your trust in Him.

What small thing can you hand over and trust God with right now, today?

_____

_____

_____

_____

_____

_____

_____

_____

_____

_____

_____

Scripture says, *lean on, trust in, and be confident in the Lord with all your heart and mind and do not rely on your own insight or understanding.*

Write a prayer asking God to help you trust Him when you are riddled with doubt.

_____

_____

_____

_____

_____

_____

_____

_____

_____

_____

_____

_____

_____

_____

_____

_____

_____

ASK HIM

...to help you gently guide the people you hoped would be supportive. Sometimes they just don't know what to say and how to be there for you.

It's happened hasn't it? Someone, whom you expected would be there to support and help you through this whole ordeal, hasn't. Their absence has left you hurt and disappointed, maybe even angry.

People don't let us down; it's our expectations we have for them that let us down. Remember, people don't always know how to handle difficult situations appropriately. Human nature consists of a mixture of both care and carelessness.

The last thing someone who cares about you wants to do is hurt you. Please don't let this situation undo an important relationship in your life.

The reason they aren't there for you could be because they honestly don't know how to be.

Cancer teaches you that life is too short to waste on misunderstandings. Reach out and guide people; let them know how they can help. *You will both* be so grateful you did.

PROVERBS 19:11

Good sense makes a man restrain his anger, and it is his glory to overlook a transgression or an offense. (AMP)

1 PETER 3:8-9

Finally, all [of you] should be of one and the same mind (united in spirit), sympathizing [with one another], loving [each other] as brethren [of one household], compassionate and courteous (tenderhearted and humble). Never return evil for evil or insult for insult (scolding, tongue-lashing, berating), but on the contrary blessing [praying for their welfare, happiness, and protection, and truly pitying and loving them]. For know that to this you have been called, that you may yourselves inherit a blessing [from God—that you may obtain a blessing as heirs, bringing welfare and happiness and protection]. (AMP)

Journal

Write a letter in your journal to anyone who you thought would have been supportive and hasn't been.

Write why it hurts, why you feel disappointed, what you expected, and why you needed them to be there for you.

Together, you and God can rise above the hurt and bring restoration to those relationships. What do you need to do?

_____

_____

_____

_____

_____

_____

_____

_____

_____

_____

_____

_____

_____

_____

People don't let us down, it's our expectations of them that let us down. That's a pretty thought provoking statement, right?

We are all at different stages in life, and you can't force someone to be further along on their journey than they are.

You can only pray for them. For whom do you need to pray? Who else do you need to let off the hook?

_____

_____

_____

_____

_____

_____

_____

_____

_____

_____

_____

_____

_____

ASK HIM

...for His divine anointing to flow through every dedicated doctor, every devoted nurse, and every researcher working to find a cure.

Today we are asking God to gather up all the people who have dedicated their time, talent, and treasure in helping people with cancer.

For His divine anointing to bless, protect, and empower each and every one of them in every aspect of their lives.

To fortify them with resilient energy and unimaginable strength as they work tirelessly for this cause.

To keep them enthusiastic as they pursue the newest and most reliable treatments and technology.

To instill in them the unwavering commitment to persevere in the face of adversity as they work to find a cure.

PSALM 20:1-6

May the Lord answer you when you are in distress; may the name of the God of Jacob protect you. May he send you help from the sanctuary and grant you support from Zion. May he remember all your sacrifices and accept your burnt offerings. May he give you the desire of your heart and make all your plans succeed. We will shout for joy when you are victorious and will lift up our banners in the name of our God. May the Lord grant all your requests. Now I know that the Lord saves his anointed. (NIV)

HEBREWS 6:10-11

God is not unjust; he will not forget your work and the love you have shown him as you have helped his people and continue to help them. We want each of you to show this same diligence to the very end, so that what you hope for may be fully realized. (NIV)

Journal

Write down some of the names of the staff members, nurses, and doctors for whom you are grateful.

Beside each name write the reasons you feel that they have made a difference in your life.

_____

_____

_____

_____

_____

_____

_____

_____

_____

_____

_____

_____

_____

_____

_____

_____

_____

_____

Looking back on your list, write down how you might honor each of them by incorporating their positive qualities into how you will treat other people in the future.

(It would be a lovely gesture to share your feelings with these special people by writing a note with the results of this exercise to express your appreciation for their positive impact on your life at such a difficult time.)

ASK HIM

...to help you harness the inner strength your body generates when it works from a position of gratitude.

Approaching life from a position of gratitude sparks inspiration and enthusiasm. When you write down the things you're grateful for, you make a conscious decision to engage the mind, heart, and spirit to something of greater value. The strength comes from the affirming influence these feelings have on your sense of well-being.

You can learn how to recognize gratitude in the very things that cause upset, the things you struggle with, in the disappointments, when you're frustrated or disillusioned, when you've failed, or when you're worried. Pursuing gratitude regardless of what conditions you're surrounded by uncovers an inner strength, a persevering strength, and a fighting spirit that will astonish even you.

When your mind is focused on gratitude, it boosts your body's ability to recover and renew itself.

Being grateful is a choice, one that can change your life. Harness its power.

COLOSSIANS 2:6-7

So then, just as you received Christ Jesus as Lord, continue to live your lives in him, rooted and built up in him, strengthened in the faith as you were taught, and over-flowing with thankfulness. (NIV)

1 THESSALONIANS 5:18

Whatever happens, always be thankful. This is how God wants you to live in Christ Jesus. (ERV)

Journal

Write down three things you are grateful for today. Then come back to this page *every day* and add one more thing to the list.

_____

_____

_____

_____

_____

_____

_____

_____

_____

_____

_____

_____

_____

_____

_____

_____

_____

_____

_____

Learning to be grateful in times of trouble can be very difficult.

Can you think of a time or two when you've struggled yet became a better person for having gone through it?

Write down all the ways God might be able to use what you are experiencing in your struggle right now to teach you something, give you wisdom, and make you stronger.

_____

_____

_____

_____

_____

_____

_____

_____

_____

_____

_____

_____

_____

ASK HIM

...to remind you that one of life's greatest achievements is bringing people to Him.

Cancer or no cancer, we all want to make a difference in this world, to leave a lasting impression.

We all want to positively impact the people we come in contact with.

Having cancer intuitively triggers an incredible sense of urgency in the matter.

The questions you might ask yourself here are: Whom exactly are you trying to impress? Is what you want to do going to make a difference in the world? What are the short and long-term benefits of achieving the success you're working so hard for? How will it impact people around you?

God wants you to succeed in being an instrument for Him in someone else's life.

Every day God works overtime setting up appointments for you.

Every day you have the power to bring someone to Him.

Every day *you* have the power to impact *someone else's forever*!

Remember, being the world to one person is the most extraordinary way to be just one person in the world.

MATTHEW 5:14-16

You are the light of the world. A city set on a mountain cannot be hidden. Nor do they light a lamp and then put it under a bushel basket; it is set on a lamp stand, where it gives light to all in the house. Just so, your light must shine before others, that they may see your good deeds and glorify your heavenly Father. (NAB)

COLOSSIANS 3:23-24

"Work willingly at whatever you do, as though you were working for the Lord rather than for people. Remember that the Lord will give you an inheritance as your reward, and that the Master you are serving is Christ." (NIV)

Journal

Who has God used as an instrument to bring you closer to Him?

List the people who have had some kind of spiritual impact on you.

What did they do or say? How did it change you?

_____

_____

_____

_____

_____

_____

_____

_____

_____

_____

_____

_____

_____

_____

_____

_____

One of life's greatest achievements is positively impacting someone else's life. Have you ever thought about impacting someone else's forever?

Sometimes having cancer opens a door to reach people you couldn't reach otherwise. Be aware of this opportunity. Write down a few life events or circumstances you could share that would help bring someone closer to God. Are there any tools you feel you might lack that could prevent you from accomplishing this? (Don't skip this part—you'll need this list in the next exercise.)

_____

_____

_____

_____

_____

_____

_____

_____

_____

_____

ASK HIM

...to remind you that on the days your cancer is too much for you, *rest assured it isn't too much for* Him!

Is today one of those dreaded days when fatigue has invaded every inch of your being?

Are you sick and tired of being sick and tired? Are you exhausted from fighting with your emotions, your body, your attitude, and your spirit? Do you dream about someone magically coming in and taking over your body so you can run away and escape this every-single-day battle?

Do you wonder how you'll keep up this exhausting fight?

It's on days like this God wants you to remember something extremely critical. When you feel like your cancer is too much for you, rest assured that it isn't too much for Him.

The Lord God Almighty is His name. Nothing is too hard for Him.

2 CORINTHIANS 10:3-5

We live in this world, but we don't fight our battles in the same way the world does. The weapons we use are not human ones. Our weapons have power from God and can destroy the enemy's strong places. We destroy people's arguments, and we tear down every proud idea that raises itself against the knowledge of God. We also capture every thought and make it give up and obey Christ. (ERV)

JEREMIAH 32:17

"Ah, Sovereign Lord, you have made the heavens and the earth by your great power and outstretched arm. Nothing is too hard for you." (NIV)

Journal

Before we go any further, we need to go back to that list you made of the things you felt you lacked that could prevent you from impacting someone else's forever. Remember?

Now take your pen and put a line through each of them—scratch them all out! God never asks you to do anything for Him unless He has equipped you with everything you need to do His will. You are fully equipped. Carry on!

Now, we can officially move on to this journal page. Go back and reread page 66. Why is your cancer too much for you today? What part of this fight is the hardest for you? Is it the relentless battle? Fear? Exhaustion?

_____

_____

_____

_____

_____

_____

_____

_____

_____

_____

On the days when your cancer is too much, you have a powerful ally in God.

You just have to find how best to channel His mighty power. For me, Praise and Worship music can break down and capture every overpowering thought and make those thoughts, like it says in the scripture on page 67, *"give up and obey God."*

There are amazing songs out there that can bring you from a bitter place to a better place. (Email me if you need help—info@askhimbooks.com.)

Make a list of your favorite songs.

_____

_____

_____

_____

_____

_____

_____

_____

_____

_____

ASK HIM

...to help you understand the significant distinction of *choosing* the mindset that you are living *with* cancer not dying *from* cancer.

Cancer will not take you from this earth. God will take you from this earth. So until He decides when that day will be, you have some decision making to do.

How do you want to live out your life here on earth? Will you wake up and go about your day *living* or *dying*?

Choosing to live intentionally despite your cancer is a mindset that will make an enormous impact on everything you do from this moment forward.

Everyday you wake up alive is a day God has specifically chosen for you. Living with cancer is about embracing today without regard for tomorrow. It savors time, guards energy, and makes deliberate choices concerning both. It holds onto hope and utterly refuses to let cancer decide.

It's an enhanced understanding of reality, offering an enhanced perspective about life.

Remember, you may have cancer but cancer doesn't have you! Choose life!

JOB 33:28

"God has delivered me from going down to the pit, and I shall live to enjoy the light of life."

2 CORINTHIANS 4:16-17

Therefore we do not become discouraged (utterly spiritless, exhausted, and wearied out through fear). Though our outer man is [progressively] decaying and wasting away, yet our inner self is being [progressively] renewed day after day. (AMP) For our light and momentary troubles are achieving for us an eternal glory that far outweighs them all. (NIV)

Journal

Are you letting cancer decide?

How are you going to approach life? Are you going to be "living with" or are you going to be "dying from" cancer?

To "live" with cancer offers an ability to love with greater intensity and to encounter a depth of feeling you never thought possible.

List some other differences that clearly make *living with* cancer the best option.

_____

_____

_____

_____

_____

_____

_____

_____

_____

_____

_____

Some would have you believe that you are dying because you have cancer.

This is a lie! Cancer doesn't decide!

What are some specific things you can do to stay focused on "living"?

_____

_____

_____

_____

_____

_____

_____

_____

_____

_____

_____

_____

_____

_____

_____

_____

ASK HIM

...for the grace to be
what inspires others.

You know those people in your life who make you feel really good just being around them? Their words are affirming, kind, compassionate, and always encouraging. You feel worthy and valued in their presence. They inspire in you new ways of embracing change, loving more patiently, giving more generously, and forgiving more easily.

These kinds of people radiate warmth, and they have an ability to instill in you a sense of peace and contentment.

So what exactly is it that these people have? They have and live in the abundance of God's grace.

Grace is unmerited favor from God. It is God perfecting in you everything you need to do good works that are pleasing in His sight.

Get to know the God who loves beautifully so you will have the grace to beautifully love.

1 PETER 4:10-11

God has shown you his grace in many different ways. So be good servants and use whatever gift he has given you in a way that will best serve each other. If your gift is speaking, your words should be like words from God. If your gift is serving, you should serve with the strength that God gives. Then it is God who will be praised in everything through Jesus Christ. Power and glory belong to him forever and ever. Amen. (ERV)

HEBREWS 10:24

We should think about each other to see how we can encourage each other to show love and do good works. (ERV)

Journal

What inspires you?

Describe three of the most memorable times when you were inspired by someone or something.

_____

_____

_____

_____

_____

_____

_____

_____

_____

_____

_____

_____

_____

_____

_____

_____

_____

_____

Have you ever been told that what you did or said was inspirational? What happened?

How did it affect the person you inspired?

How does it feel knowing that it was God's grace working through you?

_____

_____

_____

_____

_____

_____

_____

_____

_____

_____

_____

_____

_____

_____

_____

ASK HIM

...to keep the emotionally draining "What if?" and "Why me?" voices from undermining your faith and stealing your joy.

"What if?" and "Why me?" thoughts are perfectly normal. The trouble comes when these thoughts undermine your faith and overpower your ability to maintain any semblance of peace and joy. Sometimes the root cause of why these thoughts overwhelm and drain you emotionally have to do with separating which thoughts are realistically manageable and which ones you have no control over.

Turmoil and confusion are instant indicators that you're desperately trying to manage both. This emotional tug-of-war is a universal struggle, but it's also a struggle you can win. Expressing your emotions instead of keeping them churning inside lowers stress and promotes mental and physical health.

Pay attention to your feelings. One way to help you cope with some of these thoughts is to get them out of your head and onto paper. Make the decision right now to manage only what you can and let God take the rest.

Recapture God's genuine joy and authentic peace.

PSALM 42:11

Why am I so sad? Why am I so upset? I tell myself, "Wait for God's help! You will again be able to praise him, your God, the one who will save you." (ERV)

HEBREWS 11:1

Now faith is being sure of what we hope for and certain of what we do not see. (NIV)

Journal

Write a list of your most distressing "What if?" and "Why Me?" thoughts.

Next to each one write an "M" if it is something you have the ability to *manage*, or a "G" if you need to give it to *God*.

_____

_____

_____

_____

_____

_____

_____

_____

_____

_____

_____

_____

_____

_____

_____

_____

_____

By the authority of God's Word, you have the power to cast out every spirit of fear or intimidation that strikes at the foundations of your faith.

What actions can you take to recapture the genuine joy and authentic peace that the "What if?" and "Why Me?" game keeps trying to steal from you?

_____

_____

_____

_____

_____

_____

_____

_____

_____

_____

_____

_____

_____

_____

ASK HIM

...to remind you that a heart shaped by scripture yields a spirit nourished by hope.

Scripture says, *"For everything that was written in the past was written to teach us, so that through the endurance taught in the Scriptures and the encouragement they provide we might have hope"* (Rom. 15:4).

What you do when you read the scriptures is feed your spirit.

What *God* does when you read the scriptures is help the words breathe life into your spirit.

In other words, simple hope becomes God's living hope in you.

So when your heart is shaped by scripture, two things happen: First, you are nourished and encouraged by the transforming words in scripture. Second, you have an opportunity to "become hope" for people who are lost and can't find their way.

Be transformed!

ROMANS 15:4

For whatever was thus written in former days was written for our instruction, that by [our steadfast and patient] endurance and the encouragement [drawn] from the Scriptures we might hold fast to and cherish hope. (AMP)

ROMANS 15:13

I pray that the God who gives hope will fill you with much joy and peace as you trust in him. Then you will have more and more hope, and it will flow out of you by the power of the Holy Spirit. (ERV)

Journal

In this book, *ASK HIM for Courage with Cancer,* the scripture verses are written out for you.

How has reading them helped shape your heart and nourish your spirit? Has reading them helped to transform you?

_____

_____

_____

_____

_____

_____

_____

_____

_____

_____

_____

_____

_____

_____

Which scriptures have helped to transform you into a living hope and source of encouragement for other people? What are you doing differently?

_____

_____

_____

_____

_____

_____

_____

_____

_____

_____

_____

_____

_____

_____

_____

_____

_____

_____

ASK HIM

...to help you keep your eyes
focused on the path ahead, so you
don't get tripped up looking back on
what "used to be."

When your life suddenly changes in ways you wished it wouldn't, it's all you can do not to think about how it used to be.

When you have cancer you often get caught up, even fixated, on how your life was B.C. (before cancer).

Although this is not unusual, continuously dwelling on these thoughts can be terribly counterproductive. Why? Because when you're focused on what used to be, you interrupt your ability to be invested in right now.

Looking back on what used to be deprives you of the experiences God has for you up ahead. In other words, you won't ever know what's ahead if you don't persevere through *now*.

When you live in the fullness of reality, you live in the wisdom of truth.

God has a purpose for you. Try to discover and honor that purpose.

ISAIAH 43:18-19

So don't remember what happened in earlier times. Don't think about what happened a long time ago, because I am doing something new! Now you will grow like a new plant. Surely you know this is true. I will even make a road in the desert, and rivers will flow through that dry land. (ERV)

PHILIPPIANS 3:12-14

I don't mean that I am exactly what God wants me to be. I have not yet reached that goal. But I continue trying to reach it and make it mine. That's what Christ Jesus wants me to do. It is the reason he made me his. Brothers and sisters, I know that I still have a long way to go. But there is one thing I do: I forget what is in the past and try as hard as I can to reach the goal before me. I keep running hard toward the finish line to get the prize that is mine because God has called me through Christ Jesus to life up there in heaven. (ERV)

Journal

You won't find the answers behind you because God is busy doing something new in you *now*. When you live in the fullness of reality, you live in the wisdom of truth. What is one way you can stay grounded and invested in today?

_____

_____

_____

_____

_____

_____

_____

_____

_____

_____

_____

_____

_____

_____

_____

_____

When everything behind you is familiar, the road less traveled can seem scarier, but God never shuts one door without opening another. What new doors, even if different and unfamiliar, have opened since your diagnosis?

_____

_____

_____

_____

_____

_____

_____

_____

_____

_____

_____

_____

_____

_____

_____

_____

ASK HIM

...if He'd exchange every dose of treatment that makes you sick for a dose of courage and hope to someone in despair.

Have you ever thought about being able to take something awful and turn it around into something good?

Well, you can. What I have in mind is not only something extremely inspiring but it might make having to endure the unpleasant side of your cancer treatments a little easier.

I'd like to propose that you ask God for a little deal, a little trade-off, a little exchange of sorts.

ASK HIM that for every dose of treatment, which is unpleasant and makes you sick, if He'd give a dose of courage and hope to someone in despair.

To be able to recognize in your own struggle that there are other people struggling alongside you is to personify merciful compassion. It gives a noble intention to your personal affliction. It is to offer up your own suffering for the well being of another human being. It's an ultimate act of self-sacrifice. It's ordinary people doing extraordinary things.

Be extraordinary!

ROMANS 5:2-5

Through our faith, Christ has brought us into that blessing of God's grace that we now enjoy. And we are very happy because of the hope we have of sharing God's glory. And we are also happy with the troubles we have. Why are we happy with troubles? Because we know that these troubles make us more patient. And this patience is proof that we are strong. And this proof gives us hope. And this hope will never disappoint us. We know this because God has poured out his love to fill our hearts through the Holy Spirit he gave us. (ERV)

1 PETER 4:1,19

Christ suffered while he was in his body. So you should strengthen yourselves with the same kind of thinking Christ had. The one who accepts suffering in this life has clearly decided to stop sinning. So if God wants you to suffer, you should trust your lives to him. He is the one who made you, and you can trust him. So continue to do good. (ERV)

Journal

To offer up your own suffering for the well-being of another person is an extraordinary way to give a noble intention to your own affliction.

Write a list of every single annoying, miserable thing you have to go through, deal with, and endure as a result of cancer.

Next to each one, write down the name of a person you know who may need a bit of courage or hope.

For every affliction you must endure, offer God your suffering in exchange for His abundant blessings on the lives of those on your list.

_____

_____

_____

_____

_____

_____

_____

_____

_____

_____

What are you praying and hoping God will do in the lives of the people for whom you have offered up your suffering?

_____

_____

_____

_____

_____

_____

_____

_____

_____

_____

_____

_____

_____

_____

_____

_____

_____

_____

_____

ASK HIM

...if He would instill in you the courage to consider suffering as a means to a profoundly deeper unity with Him.

Jesus was both fully human and fully divine. Because He encountered indescribable depths of human suffering, more than anyone, He is able to uniquely understand the depths in which you suffer.

It is precisely because of His understanding and experience of suffering that He wants to be united with you in your suffering. A special bond forms between people who have a shared experience of suffering.

That bond in suffering is where God seeks you. He knows suffering is a place where hearts are fused, where unity diffuses pain, where comfort can be found in discomfort. He knows that this frightening and unfamiliar place is where He can be there for you and forge a deeper and more profound unity with you.

At a time when you need God the most, He's there, offering an extravagant expression of divine grace so that, like Him, you will be fortified and able to bear the cross and hardship of suffering with dignity and perseverance.

HEBREWS 2:18

For because He Himself [in His humanity] has suffered in being tempted (tested and tried), He is able [immediately] to run to the cry of (assist, relieve) those who are being tempted and tested and tried [and who therefore are being exposed to suffering]. (AMP)

1 PETER 5:10

Yes, you will suffer for a short time. But after that, God will make everything right. He will make you strong. He will support you and keep you from falling. He is the God who gives all grace. He chose you to share in his glory in Christ. That glory will continue forever. (ERV)

Journal

On the cross, Jesus cried out, "My God, My God, why have you abandoned me?"

Have you ever been angry or felt abandoned by God in your suffering? Tell Him!

_____

_____

_____

_____

_____

_____

_____

_____

_____

_____

_____

_____

_____

_____

Go back and read the two scripture verses on page 95. God doesn't promise you will live a life free of suffering. He promises He will immediately run to the cry of those suffering.

Does this promise console you? How?

_____

_____

_____

_____

_____

_____

_____

_____

_____

_____

_____

_____

_____

_____

_____

ASK HIM

...to remind you that there's *power*, not weakness, in surrendering your circumstances and trusting your outcome to Him.

We all know and understand that the word *surrender* implies powerlessness and defeat.

So I guess to ask you if you would be willing to surrender your life and your circumstances to someone else might seem a little absurd. But wait! To surrender your life and circumstances to God is altogether different.

With God, there is great power, not weakness, in surrender. When you surrender to God, you are yielding to the power of the great I Am. He's the Alpha and the Omega, the beginning and the end, the One who placed each planet in its galaxy and positioned each star in the sky.

This act of self-surrender alters everything.

It's giving up your human power, so the One with the divine power can be your advocate and strength.

Never, ever underestimate the considerable difference between mortal strength and spiritual strength.

Go ahead...wave the white flag!

Trust me, it's a win-win!

ACTS 11:21

And the presence of the Lord was with them with power, so that a great number [learned] to believe (to adhere to and trust in and rely on the Lord) and turned and surrendered themselves to Him. (AMP)

1 THESSALONIANS 2:13

And we also [especially] thank God continually for this, that when you received the message of God [which you heard] from us, you welcomed it not as the word of [mere] men, but as it truly is, the Word of God, which is effectually at work in you who believe [exercising its superhuman power in those who adhere to and trust in and rely on it]. (AMP)

Journal

Do you consider yourself powerful? Are you physically strong? Mentally strong? Spiritually strong? Where is your power source?

What do you think divine power can do that human power can't?

_____

_____

_____

_____

_____

_____

_____

_____

_____

_____

_____

_____

_____

_____

Close your eyes and imagine the calm and relief you would feel to no longer shoulder being completely and utterly responsible. *That's* what it feels like to surrender; when you can accept and trust His plan, no matter the outcome.

How can you begin, a little each day, to surrender your uncertainty and replace it with the strength to trust?

_____

_____

_____

_____

_____

_____

_____

_____

_____

_____

_____

_____

_____

ASK HIM

...to help your family and friends understand how tremendously reassuring it is to be around other cancer survivors who've already "walked in your shoes."

Dynamics within relationships can become tricky when someone has cancer. There becomes a delicate balance between family and friends who want you to go to them for comfort and encouragement, and your wanting and needing to be around other cancer survivors who've already "walked in your shoes."

It's hard for them to truly understand the notion that if it were humanly possible, you would track down and meet every single person who has ever had your type of cancer, walked through it, and *survived!*

You don't have to explain that to other survivors; they get it. Of course, this doesn't mean that your family and friends *don't* get it. It's just that people who have walked in your shoes get it on a whole different level. Cancer and relationships can sometimes be tricky but what sustains them is thoughtful, gentle love that's rooted in understanding. Remember..."Love above all." – *Jean de Dieu Musabyiamana*

ROMANS 15:5

Now may the God Who gives the power of patient endurance (steadfastness) and Who supplies encouragement, grant you to live in such mutual harmony and such full sympathy with one another, in accord with Christ Jesus. (AMP)

COLOSSIANS 3:12,14

Therefore, as God's chosen people, holy and dearly loved, clothe yourselves with compassion, kindness, humility, gentleness and patience. And over all these virtues put on love, which binds them all together in perfect unity. (NIV)

Journal

How does it help you when you meet other survivors who've already walked in your shoes?

What have they shared that gave you the biggest source of comfort?

_____

_____

_____

_____

_____

_____

_____

_____

_____

_____

_____

_____

_____

_____

_____

What relationships have most notably changed since your diagnosis? Are they stronger? Are they strained?

The scripture specifically says *clothe* yourselves with compassion, kindness, humility, gentleness, and patience. And over all these virtues put on love, which binds them all together in perfect unity.

Think about how some honest communication fortified by this scripture could help you in your relationships. Who do you need to speak to? What do you want to say?

ASK HIM

...to remind you when your prayers
have limitations, you're denying Him
a chance to do miraculous things.

We do it all the time, and we don't even realize it. While praying, we often unknowingly put God in a box.

When we pray with our own self-imposed restrictions, we are limiting God's response to us.

How many times have you made your requests known to God, then provided Him with advice on how best He should handle them?

Are you concerned He won't be able to solve the problem or find a solution? Maybe you think it's fruitless to ask God for things that are out of reach, unattainable, or unrealistic. But that's exactly what God wants you to ask for!

Thinking something is impossible for God takes Him out of the equation because you limit His ability. We *can't* let our minds limit what God can do for us!

Ask for the impossible. Your God is a God of endless possibilities with unlimited resources. He can make possible what the world thinks is impossible.

Pray big. Ask for the unimaginable. Believe in the unbelievable!

LUKE 11:9-10

"And I tell you, ask and you will receive; seek and you will find; knock and the door will be opened to you. For everyone who asks, receives; and the one who seeks, finds; and to the one who knocks, the door will be opened." (NAB)

EPHESIANS 3:20

Now to Him Who, by [in consequence of] the [action of His] power that is at work within us, is able to [carry out His purpose and] do superabundantly, far over and above all that we [dare] ask or think [infinitely beyond our highest prayers, desires, thoughts, hopes, or dreams]. (AMP)

Journal

Ask for the impossible. Your God is a God of endless possibilities with unlimited resources. He can make possible what the world thinks is impossible. *Pray big!* Ask for the unimaginable. Believe in the unbelievable.

Write out a prayer to God with no limitations. Repeat it every day!

_____

_____

_____

_____

_____

_____

_____

_____

_____

_____

_____

_____

_____

_____

Have you subconsciously kept God in a box?

Have you lost faith?

Write a prayer asking God to give you unshakeable faith to wholeheartedly believe the scripture on page 107—Ephesians 3:20. Repeat it every day!

_____

_____

_____

_____

_____

_____

_____

_____

_____

_____

_____

_____

_____

_____

ASK HIM

...to gather you into God's soothing providence when you're feeling the most discouraged.

Discouragement can get in the way and prevent you from being able to see things with clarity. It feeds on the negative effects of earthly circumstances.

Discouragement will stand idly by when disappointments flood into your heart and mind. It prevents you from being able to see beyond the circumstances.

God knows this. He also knows that this is when you're most tempted to give up.

He has a better plan.

He wants to gather you into His soothing providence where you can just sit and rest a while.

Let Him shine His light into the dark corners of discouragement. Let Him refresh your withered spirit.

Be immersed in His protective love. Know that He is with you, the wind beneath your wings, for as long as it takes, until you've regained your strength...until you've renewed your confidence...until your spirit has been restored.

PSALM 91:1-4

Whoever dwells in the shelter of the Most High will rest in the shadow of the Almighty. He will cover you with his feathers, and under his wings you will find refuge; his faithfulness will be your shield and rampart. (NIV)

MATTHEW 11:28-30

Come to Me, all you who labor and are heavy-laden and overburdened, and I will cause you to rest. [I will ease and relieve and refresh your souls.] Take My yoke upon you and learn of Me, for I am gentle (meek) and humble (lowly) in heart, and you will find rest (relief and ease and refreshment and recreation and blessed quiet) for your souls. For My yoke is wholesome (useful, good—not harsh, hard, sharp, or pressing, but comfortable, gracious, and pleasant), and My burden is light and easy to be borne. (AMP)

Journal

Are there particular situations or circumstances when you feel especially discouraged? Identify a few here.

_____

_____

_____

_____

_____

_____

_____

_____

_____

_____

_____

_____

_____

_____

_____

_____

_____

_____

_____

When you are discouraged, God calls you to draw near to Him, deep where His heart beats. He wants you to stay awhile so He can care for you. He wants to be with you until your withered spirit begins to feel refreshed.

Think back to when you were young and a parent or grandparent would scoop you up and hold you close and tight. Remember how comforting that was?

Reread Matthew 11:28-30 on page 111.

ASK HIM

...to help you confidently own the statement: My cancer cannot and will not define me!

Cancer got your attention! All of a sudden, everything about you, around you, and connected to you centers around *the cancer*.

Your very identity begins to get swallowed up in it all.

You're even having a hard time remembering who you were B.C. (before cancer).

Stop here!

Even if every thing I just said is true, *cancer cannot and will not define you!*

You are defined by the way you choose to face the circumstances of your life.

You are defined by your ability to approach every phase of your life as an opportunity to grow and develop into someone more compassionate, more tolerant, more loving, more trusting, and more faithful.

This is about standing firm with confidence that you define yourself by who you are and by who God created you to be *not* by some disease you have.

EPHESIANS 2:10

For we are God's [own] handiwork (His workmanship), recreated in Christ Jesus, [born anew] that we may do those good works which God predestined (planned beforehand) for us [taking paths which He prepared ahead of time], that we should walk in them [living the good life which He pre-arranged and made ready for us to live]. (AMP)

HEBREWS 10:39

But we do not belong to those who shrink back and are destroyed, but to those who have faith and are saved. (NIV)

Journal

What are you known for? How do people describe you? What defines you?

Transfer that information to several index cards.

Tape one to your bathroom mirror, one on the refrigerator, and one on the dashboard of your car. Use these as visible reminders of your truth.

_____

_____

_____

_____

_____

_____

_____

_____

_____

_____

_____

_____

You know this disease does not define you.

If your identity has been inadvertently consumed by all the cancer commotion, what can you do to reclaim your sense of self?

_____

_____

_____

_____

_____

_____

_____

_____

_____

_____

_____

_____

_____

_____

ASK HIM

...to intervene when you're tired so you don't take your frustrations out on the people you love the most.

I know that the last thing you ever thought you'd have to do is tell the people you love that you have cancer.

Everyone's life changes that day. Technically speaking, everyone gets cancer that day.

The cancer may be *physically* in your body, but it's *emotionally* in theirs.

The family will begin the fight, but you will begin the war. Your war requires everything you have, every day, whether you're tired or hurting or not.

You spend so much energy and emotion as a warrior, there is not much left at the end of the day.

Well that is.....*except friends and family*! And sometimes these very people are the ones who become the easiest targets when you're overtired.

Ask Him if He sees you about to say or do something you might regret, to intervene so you don't unintentionally hurt the people you're trying so hard to love the most.

PSALMS 73:26

My flesh and my heart may fail, but God is the strength of my heart and my portion forever. (NIV)

EPHESIANS 4:2-3

Always be humble and gentle. Be patient and accept each other with love. You are joined together with peace through the Spirit. Do all you can to continue as you are, letting peace hold you together. (ERV)

Journal

When you are repeatedly overtired, it affects your ability to function and interact in many ways.

Write down what you are going through right now that is causing the most distress. Can anyone help? *Ask!*

Sometimes your family and friends become the easiest targets when you're frustrated and overtired.

Remember, Psalm 73:26 says; *"Your flesh and your heart may fail; but God is the strength of your heart forever."*

With the strength of God's heart, take some time to go back and apologize to anyone you may have hurt when you were frustrated and overtired.

ASK HIM

...to remind you that the way to fix a regretful yesterday is to seize every opportunity today.

Everyone has those days they wish they could do over, but yesterday is already gone so you'll need to refocus your attention on making the most you can with today.

When you view regrets and disappointments as negatives, you take away an important chance to learn more about yourself.

I bet you wouldn't be so quick to avoid looking at your weaknesses if you believed those weaknesses were merely strengths "in training," would you?

You have to begin accepting the reality that it's not a matter of "if" you'll mess up. It's a matter of "when" and the magnitude of the mess! We all mess up. It's inevitable.

The goal is powerfully simple—acquire more wisdom today than yesterday.

If you have regrets about something that happened yesterday, just always endeavor to do the next right thing. It makes life so much less complicated.

Let go of the regrets of yesterday and seize today!

JEREMIAH 29:11

For I know well the plans I have in mind for you, says the Lord, plans for your welfare, and not for woe! plans to give you a future full of hope. (NAB)

GALATIANS 6:9

Let us not become weary in doing good, for at the proper time we will reap a harvest if we do not give up. (NIV)

Journal

You can't change the past, but you can take the lessons you learned in the past and let them change your future.

List some lessons you've learned in your past that have positively changed your future.

_____

_____

_____

_____

_____

_____

_____

_____

_____

_____

_____

_____

_____

_____

_____

_____

Every moment in life can be viewed as an opportunity.
Even if you didn't have a regrettable yesterday, what
opportunities has God set before you today?

_____

_____

_____

_____

_____

_____

_____

_____

_____

_____

_____

_____

_____

_____

_____

_____

_____

_____

_____

ASK HIM

...for the indescribable comfort that comes from believing He will continue to take care of the people you love the most.

You contemplate a lot of different things when you have cancer. One of the most dreaded is: what if I don't make it?

Most of our anguish about death comes with the realization that our physical presence will no longer be able to love, influence, and celebrate the people we love the most, but it also comes with the painful awareness that our death will be the cause of heartbreak and grief in the lives of those we love.

Death is out of our control. In order to find a sense of comfort, we must try to understand the process and prepare for it.

Indescribable comfort can be found when you believe in the deepest part of your soul that God will fill that void for the people you leave behind. He also promised you that death does not mean *the end* for you or someone you love.

Death is a temporary separation we are called to endure until we are reunited again in eternity. Let the peace of this promise wash over and comfort you.

EZEKIEL 34:11-12

The Lord God says, "I myself will be their Shepherd. I will search for my sheep and take care of them. If a shepherd is with his sheep when they begin to wander away, he will go searching for them. In the same way I will search for my sheep. I will save them and bring them back from all the places where they were scattered on that dark and cloudy day. (ERV)

JOHN 17:15-19

My prayer is not that you take them out of the world but that you protect them from the evil one. They are not of the world, even as I am not of it. Sanctify them by the truth; your word is truth. As you sent me into the world, I have sent them into the world. For them I sanctify myself, that they too may be truly sanctified. (NIV)

Journal

Just as you will be with God, God will be with those you leave behind too. You are mistaken if you think that no one can love like you do. God can! Leaving the people you love in the hands of God is leaving them to be gloriously, super-naturally, and divinely loved.

Use this page to write special love notes to the people who are most important in your life.

_____

_____

_____

_____

_____

_____

_____

_____

_____

_____

_____

_____

_____

_____

_____

God gave us the capacity to love with enormous intensity; therefore when we know we will be separated in death from the people we love, it hurts with enormous intensity as well.

God also knows that with every end comes a new kind of beginning for those left behind.

Express to God what are the five things that frighten you the most. Who would you like for God to take particularly special care of? Why?

How can He help you find the courage to entrust to Him the ones you love the most?

_____

_____

_____

_____

_____

_____

_____

_____

_____

_____

ASK HIM

...if He is all-powerful and all-knowing, why He would let such a thing like cancer happen to you.

This is what is so difficult to understand about God—if He wanted, He could intervene and make your cancer go away in an instant. Why doesn't He? It's been said that the human person is capable of withstanding enormous despair if they can somehow explain or make the circumstances "make sense" in their brains. So when we see senseless tragedies, when we see bad things happen to really good people we wonder, where is God in all of this?

We feel rejected and betrayed by God.

The truth is, even when no satisfactory explanation exists, God exists. We are in His constant care. Somehow you must try and dig down really deep and find the courage to trust Him even when it categorically, entirely, and obviously doesn't make sense. The reason He tells you in scripture not to lean on your own understanding is because it is impossible in our human capacity to grasp the complexity of God.

There are answers to every single one of life's tragedies. Some God will reveal in our lifetimes and others won't get fully answered until we meet Him face to face.

PSALM 91:11-12, 14-15

For he will command his angels concerning you to guard you in all your ways; they will lift you up in their hands, so that you will not strike your foot against a stone. "Because he loves me," says the Lord, "I will rescue him; I will protect him, for he acknowledges my name. He will call on me, and I will answer him; I will be with him in trouble, I will deliver him and honor him. (NIV)

PSALM 34:18

The Lord is close to the brokenhearted and saves those who are crushed in spirit. (NIV)

Journal

Sometimes God's answer will be yes, and sometimes it will be no. In both instances God is saying, "This is My will for you."

"Faith is the substance of things hoped for, the evidence of things not seen."

How can you preserve your faith in the midst of unanswered questions?

What are some of the questions you're going to ask God when you meet Him face to face?

_____

_____

_____

_____

_____

_____

_____

_____

_____

_____

There will be times when you are angry at cancer.

There will be times when you are angry at God.

Is there someone you know who has gracefully dealt with extremely trying or tragic circumstances? List a couple of these people. What did you see in them that you admired? How can you emulate their example of grace under fire?

_____

_____

_____

_____

_____

_____

_____

_____

_____

_____

_____

_____

_____

ASK HIM

...to help you remember that there are *never* any relapses or setbacks greater than God.

You've done everything possible, and you've just found out that your cancer didn't respond the way it was supposed to. It seems as if every ounce of courage has drained from your body. You can't breathe. You can't stand unaided.

Defeated doesn't even begin to express how you feel.

I know that nothing I can write will magically make this go away, but what I *can* do is give you something to think about.

There is *nothing* greater than God! He tells us in scripture, *"In this world you will have trouble. But take heart! I have overcome the world!"*

Take heart means to receive courage or comfort from some fact.

God wants you to receive courage and comfort from the fact that He has overcome the world!

Let the words of Corrie ten Boom resonate within you: "No pit is so deep that He is not deeper still."

PROVERBS 21:30

There is no [human] wisdom or understanding or counsel [that can prevail] against the Lord. (AMP)

JOHN 16:33

I have told you these things, so that in Me you may have [perfect] peace and confidence. In the world you have tribulation and trials and distress and frustration; but be of good cheer [take courage; be confident, certain, undaunted]! For I have overcome the world. [I have deprived it of power to harm you and have conquered it for you.] (AMP)

Journal

God wants you to know with absolute certainty that He is greater than any relapse or setback. By fully embracing this powerful reality, you will be able to courageously stand strong against the enemy of doubt.

Make no mistake about it—doubt is cunning. It will wait patiently for the slightest sign of weakness and then try to steal the confident assurance and comfort God has intended for you.

When things don't make sense, what will you do to withstand the enemy of doubt?

John 16:33: *I have told you these things, so that in Me you may have [perfect] peace and confidence. In the world you have tribulation and trials and distress and frustration; but be of good cheer [take courage; be confident, certain, undaunted]! For I have overcome the world. [I have deprived it of power to harm you and have conquered it for you.]*

How can you live boldly in this extraordinary promise from God?

_____

_____

_____

_____

_____

_____

_____

_____

_____

_____

_____

_____

_____

ASK HIM

...to remind you that the Creator lives within His created.

You are valued and made worthy because *you* were God's motivation and inspiration. All the characteristics of the Divine Creator are in His created.

Magnificent through magnificence, love through love personified. You are perfected through perfection. You are wisdom's chosen student. It's the Prince of Peace living inside of you. Everything He is, resides in you. Scripture says that the kingdom of God is within us.

Let yourself experience the power and magnificence of the Creator living within you—His created.

Let the internal residence of your Divine Creator be marvelously apparent in who you are today.

Let your dreams be filled with eager anticipation of the endless possibilities your Creator has promised for you.

EPHESIANS 4:24

Be that new person who was made to be like God, truly good and pleasing to him. (ERV)

COLOSSIANS 3:10-11

Now you are wearing a new life, a life that is new every day. You are growing in your understanding of the one who made you. You are becoming more and more like him. In this new life it doesn't matter if you are a Greek or a Jew, circumcised or not. It doesn't matter if you speak a different language or even if you are a Scythian. It doesn't matter if you are a slave or free. Christ is all that matters, and he is in all of you. (ERV)

Journal

When you really think about the Creator of the world living inside of you, it is mind-boggling.

God is with you—before you, behind you, beside you, above you, below you, and in you!

Armed with this crucial insight, do you see yourself differently now?

Do you feel a tad more confident? Secure? Holy?

_____

_____

_____

_____

_____

_____

_____

_____

_____

_____

_____

_____

_____

Every day is new. Every day we can grow more and more like our Creator.

What parts of your Creator do you wish you were more like? Why?

_____

_____

_____

_____

_____

_____

_____

_____

_____

_____

_____

_____

_____

_____

_____

_____

_____

_____

ASK HIM

...to help you see that the bigger
truth reflected in the mirror is your
unbridled strength and courage, not
a bald head or imperfect body.

Do you think God loves you because of the way you
look? Well, just in case you're not quite sure, it is a
resounding *no*—not even close, not a chance.

He's focused on something that can't be physically seen
from the outside—your heart. What resides in your heart is
all that concerns Him.

He isn't concerned if you have scars, or if you don't have
hair, or if your body is misshapen. But make no mistake, He
knows the distress these things cause you and will never dis-
count the mental suffering you endure as a result.

He just begs you to resist the way this broken world
views what is valuable.

He begs you to see more than what is visually reflected
when you stand in front of a mirror. He wants to help you
see with His eyes the deeper truth of who you are.

He wants you to embrace the bigger truth that your
worth is solely and exclusively reflected in your heart, not in
a mirror.

I CORINTHIANS 12:21-26

The eye cannot say to the hand, "I do not need you," nor again the head to the feet, "I do not need you." Indeed, the parts of the body that seem to be weaker are all the more necessary, and those parts of the body that we consider less honorable we surround with greater honor, and our less presentable parts are treated with greater propriety, whereas our more presentable parts do not need this. But God has so constructed the body as to give greater honor to a part that is without it, so that there may be no division in the body, but that the parts may have the same concern for one another. If [one] part suffers, all the parts suffer with it; if one part is honored, all the parts share its joy. (NAB)

2 CORINTHIANS 4:16-18

Therefore we do not lose heart. Though outwardly we are wasting away, yet inwardly we are being renewed day by day. For our light and momentary troubles are achieving for us an eternal glory that far outweighs them all. So we fix our eyes not on what is seen, but on what is unseen, since what is seen is temporary, but what is unseen is eternal. (NIV)

Journal

Write down everything you see when you look in a mirror.

What do you value most? Why?

_____

_____

_____

_____

_____

_____

_____

_____

_____

_____

_____

_____

_____

_____

_____

_____

_____

_____

What are some things that you see as ugly and God may see as beautiful? Why are they ugly to you and beautiful to God?

Can you allow yourself to see the value and worthiness that God already sees in you?

_____

_____

_____

_____

_____

_____

_____

_____

_____

_____

_____

_____

_____

_____

_____

ASK HIM

...on those days when you're feeling trapped in worry and doubt, to lift you up and gently place you back in the middle of His sufficiency.

There are many days when no matter what you do, you just feel down and depressed. Your spirit feels uneasy and troubled. You feel trapped in your own negativity and can't seem to make any progress to free yourself from the tight hold it seems to have on you.

This is when you need to call for reinforcements.

God doesn't just barge in and change the way you feel. He just wants to enhance your ability to modify your condition, to amend that worry and doubt, by reminding you to be centered in His providence, His sufficiency.

Close your eyes and remember a time when you were particularly worried about something, but then finally got good news. Try and remember the tremendous feeling of relief that flooded your body. *That's* what it feels like to rest in His sufficiency.

Have faith that He is *enough*. God has a valid point when He asks, *"Who of you by worrying can add a single hour to your life?"* (Matt. 6:27)

LUKE 24:38 AND ISAIAH 44:8

And He said to them, Why are you disturbed and troubled, and why do such doubts and questionings arise in your hearts? Luke 24:39 (ERV)

"Don't be afraid! Don't worry. I am the one who always told you what would happen. You are my proof. There is no other God; I am the only one. There is no other 'Rock'; I know I am the only one." (ERV)

2 CORINTHIANS 3:4-5

Such is the reliance and confidence that we have through Christ toward and with reference to God. Not that we are fit (qualified and sufficient in ability) of ourselves to form personal judgments or to claim or count anything as coming from us, but our power and ability and sufficiency are from God. (AMP)

Journal

No matter how many times God reminds you that He's a place of refuge, He can't bring you to Himself if you won't let Him take you. Your willingness to be transported is all it takes.

How are you letting your worry and doubt ward off your more urgent need to find rest in His sufficiency?

_____

_____

_____

_____

_____

_____

_____

_____

_____

_____

_____

_____

_____

_____

God will freely and without reservation give His grace, His favor, His lovingkindness, and His mercy. He says it is sufficient against any danger and will enable you to bear what trouble comes your way.

Can you add a single hour to your life by worrying?

List the top three things you worry about that keep you up at night. Is there anything on this list that God can't handle?

How will you ever know that He is enough if you don't give Him a chance?

_____

_____

_____

_____

_____

_____

_____

_____

_____

_____

ASK HIM

...to be your steadfast source of strength and encouragement when you're feeling totally isolated in your struggle with this disease.

No one...absolutely no one can understand the complexity of emotions you go through living with this disease.

You can have the most amazing friends and the most supportive family, but at the end of the day, you are the only one who lives in your body and can fight this monster called cancer.

This is one of the most difficult and lonely realities you're faced with, and God knows it.

In scripture He says, *"So do not fear, for I am with you; do not be dismayed, for I am your God. I will strengthen you and help you. I will instruct you and teach you in the way you should go; I will counsel you with my loving eye on you."*

When you are struggling and feel totally isolated with this disease, lean on Him.

Rely on His promise to be your source of strength and encouragement.

PSALM 32:8,10

I will instruct you and teach you in the way you should go; I will counsel you with my loving eye on you. Many are the woes of the wicked, but the Lord's unfailing love surrounds the one who trusts in him. (NIV)

ISAIAH 41:10

Fear not [there is nothing to fear], for I am with you; do not look around you in terror and be dismayed, for I am your God. I will strengthen and harden you to difficulties, yes, I will help you; yes, I will hold you up and retain you with My [victorious] right hand of rightness and justice. (AMP)

Journal

Sometimes it is important to articulate or clarify how it feels when you feel isolated because of your cancer. Take a deep breath, and explain what it is like to feel totally isolated in your struggle with this disease.

_____

_____

_____

_____

_____

_____

_____

_____

_____

_____

_____

_____

_____

_____

_____

_____

God specifically addresses this issue of isolation in the scriptures on page 151. Reread them and write down how God says He's going to be there for you. What does He specifically say He is going to do to help? What do you find the most comforting when you read those scriptures?

_____

_____

_____

_____

_____

_____

_____

_____

_____

_____

_____

_____

_____

_____

_____

_____

ASK HIM

...when you feel like you can never *do* or *be* enough, to remind you, you're perfectly and completely enough for Him.

You are not expected to be perfect. But did you know that most people don't ever accomplish what they set out to do in a day?

You know why? They have totally unrealistic expectations of what is doable in a day.

So every day, these people wake up, plan their unrealistic days, and never accomplish what they think they should. Then a sense of guilt sets in. They question if they're good enough or disciplined enough.

The truth is, you *are* good enough. God designed you as a human being, not a human doing.

He adores you and accepts you for exactly who you are. There is nothing you have *to do* in order for God to love you. He loves you because you merely exist in this world not because of what you've done or not done lately.

To God, you are a precious treasure He will always cherish.

2 PETER 1:5-8

Because you have these blessings, do all you can to add to your life these things: to your faith add goodness; to your goodness add knowledge; to your knowledge add self-control; to your self-control add patience; to your patience add devotion to God; to your devotion add kindness toward your brothers and sisters in Christ, and to this kindness add love. If all these things are in you and growing, you will never fail to be useful to God. You will produce the kind of fruit that should come from your knowledge of our Lord Jesus Christ. (ERV)

EPHESIANS 3:16-19

I pray that out of his glorious riches he may strengthen you with power through his Spirit in your inner being, so that Christ may dwell in your hearts through faith. And I pray that you, being rooted and established in love, may have power, together with all the Lord's holy people, to grasp how wide and long and high and deep is the love of Christ, and to know this love that surpasses knowledge—that you may be filled to the measure of all the fullness of God. (NIV)

Journal

Are you waking up, planning unrealistic days, and never accomplishing what you think you should?

What was on your list today that didn't get done? List two things that *must* be done tomorrow and two things that, if the truth be told, you can just forget about.

_____

_____

_____

_____

_____

_____

_____

_____

_____

_____

_____

_____

_____

_____

_____

When God says you are completely loveable not because of what you do but because you merely exist, what does that mean to you?

Can you permit yourself to be enveloped by worthiness without achievement?

List *one* thing you can accomplish today merely by staying in one place, resting, and not actually *doing* something. Can you add other items or tasks to this list?

_____

_____

_____

_____

_____

_____

_____

_____

_____

_____

_____

_____

_____

_____

ASK HIM

...to remind you that when you feel the most tired, the most weary, and the most depleted, He's the most powerful.

There are no words to describe the human body when it is utterly and totally depleted. Am I right?

Did you not know? Have you not heard? God, the Creator of the ends of the earth, does not grow tired or weary. Ever!

He's made possible something absolutely astounding. When you are at your human weakest, He comes amid the extreme exhaustion in your body and releases His power so that His strength is made perfect in your weakness.

You keep thinking that being tired, weary, and depleted are problems that you must overcome.

The more drained and empty you are, the more room God has to fill you with His power and strength.

Let go and let God!

ISAIAH 40:28-31

Surely you know the truth. Surely you have heard. The Lord is the God who lives forever! He created all the faraway places on earth. He does not get tired and weary. You cannot learn all he knows. He helps tired people be strong. He gives power to those without it. Young men get tired and need to rest. Even young boys stumble and fall. But those who trust in the Lord will become strong again. They will be like eagles that grow new feathers. They will run and not get weak. They will walk and not get tired. (ERV)

2 CORINTHIANS 12:9

But He said to me, My grace (My favor and loving-kindness and mercy) is enough for you [sufficient against any danger and enables you to bear the trouble manfully]; for My strength and power are made perfect (fulfilled and completed) and show themselves most effective in [your] weakness. Therefore, I will all the more gladly glory in my weaknesses and infirmities, that the strength and power of Christ (the Messiah) may rest (yes, may pitch a tent over and dwell) upon me! (AMP)

Journal

Next time you are completely wiped out, try to remember this section and close your eyes. Think about a bicycle pump inflating a flat tire. Think about a hot air balloon slowly filling with air and rising into the sky. Think about one of those nutty inflatable characters that you see in your neighbor's yard during the holidays. Now imagine God filling *you* with His power and strength. How does it feel to have a God who wants to give you His best when you are at your worst?

_____

_____

_____

_____

_____

_____

_____

_____

_____

_____

Number your page from 1 to 15. Go back to page 159 and reread the scriptures, Isaiah 40:28-31 and 2 Corinthians 12:9. Take them apart sentence by sentence. Write everything God says and does. I've given you a head start. Read them all out when you're finished. It's pretty powerful isn't it?

1. God lives forever!
2. He created all the faraway places on earth.
3. God does not get tired or weary.
4. I cannot learn all He knows.

_____

_____

_____

_____

_____

_____

_____

_____

_____

_____

ASK HIM

...to remind you that contrary to popular belief...you *can* have cancer *and* a sense of humor.

There is something tremendously important to your overall health that you may be overlooking. It's your sense of humor, your laughter, and your silliness.

I know that you're thinking, *Get a life, Jane! Cancer and laughter don't exactly go together.* But nothing can be further from the truth.

They do go together. You *can* have cancer *and* a sense of humor *at the same time*!

God designed laughter in such a way that it sparks a chemical and physical reaction in your body that promotes healing.

Whether you feel like it or not, you need to intentionally incorporate laughter and silliness into your life.

Go to a comedy club. Get a group together and go see every funny movie that comes out in the theater. Do something ridiculously goofy. Make it happen.

Reclaiming your laughter and sense of humor might possibly be one of the most vital parts of your survivorship plan.

PROVERBS 17:22

A happy heart is good medicine and a cheerful mind works healing, but a broken spirit dries up the bones. (AMP)

JOHN 15:11

I have told you these things, that My joy and delight may be in you, and that your joy and gladness may be of full measure and complete and overflowing. (AMP)

 Journal

Have you gotten so caught up in the pressures of cancer that you've forgotten how to laugh and smile?

There is a natural healing component built into your body when you laugh.

Write out a contract with specific details of how you plan to reclaim your sense of humor and tap into that healing. Sign the contract!

_____

_____

_____

_____

_____

_____

_____

_____

_____

_____

_____

_____

_____

Don't ever let yourself underestimate the significant benefits of being totally goofy and silly.

If you start to sense even the tiniest inkling of resistance, immediately, intentionally, and with wild and reckless abandon, incorporate extraordinary measures of foolishness into your survivorship plan.

What plots or schemes of foolishness can you instigate and carry out? Write down your ideas and let the foolishness begin!

ASK HIM

...to remind you that forgiveness is a terrible thing to waste.

Forgiveness is not a feeling; it's a decision.

It isn't optional either; it's a commandment.

God's feelings about forgiveness are transparent. You have to give it to get it.

Unforgiveness has damaging affects; it mentally and emotionally holds you in the negative circumstances that created the bitterness in the first place.

It's like drinking poison and expecting the other person to die.

It's not about right and wrong. But let me be perfectly clear, forgiveness doesn't *ever* condone the actions. It just releases *you* from any hostility. It releases you from the destructive consequences the anger and resentment cause in your body.

Unforgiveness prevents healing. It blocks the vital pathways of the peace that brings restoration to your mind, body, and soul.

Don't let unforgiveness steal precious time from your life.

MATTHEW 18: 21-22

Then Peter approaching asked him, "Lord, if my brother sins against me, how often must I forgive him? As many as seven times?" Jesus answered, "I say to you, not seven times but seventy-seven times." (NAB)

1 PETER 4:8

Most important of all, love each other deeply, because love makes you willing to forgive many sins. (ERV)

Journal

Forgiveness is as simple as this: You have to give it to get it! Whom do you need to forgive?

_____

_____

_____

_____

_____

_____

_____

_____

_____

_____

_____

_____

_____

_____

_____

Has there ever been anyone who wouldn't forgive you for something you did for which you were truly sorry?

Asking for forgiveness more than once *is* allowed.

Is there anyone you need to make another effort to make amends with?

If you are hesitating, where's the hesitation coming from?

_____

_____

_____

_____

_____

_____

_____

_____

_____

_____

_____

_____

_____

_____

ASK HIM

...for the relief of knowing that God has unrestricted access in every hospital and operating room, during every scan and with every chemo and radiation treatment, so you'll *never* undergo a procedure alone...ever.

I remember sitting in the waiting room when the nurse would come get my Dad and take him away for his PET scan. I remember thinking that I wished there was some way I could go with him.

Then I started thinking about how many times and how many places in this cancer process that family and friends aren't allowed to be with you.

The last thing you want when you're vulnerable, scared and nervous is to be alone. Well, guess what? You're not!

Any time your family and friends aren't allowed to go with you, your God can! There are no rules, no restrictions, and no HIPAA concerns. He is with you everywhere you go.

He wants you to feel enveloped in His powerful presence, His steady strength, and His complete and utter desire to love you through every moment of this process...and your life. Even when alone, you are not alone!

170

DEUTERONOMY 31:8

"The Lord himself goes before you and will be with you; he will never leave you nor forsake you. Do not be afraid; do not be discouraged." (NIV)

JOSHUA 1:9

I command you: be strong and steadfast! Do not fear nor be dismayed, for the Lord, your God, is with you wherever you go. (NAB)

Journal

Next time you're sitting alone waiting, imagine it's a chilly day and a soft blanket that was just pulled from a hot dryer is wrapped around your shoulders. When you are alone, that's the kind of warmth God wants you to feel from His presence. Tell God about the times when you feel most alone in the cancer process? Most vulnerable? Most apprehensive? Feel the warmth of His presence.

_____

_____

_____

_____

_____

_____

_____

_____

_____

_____

_____

_____

Faith requires you to walk, not by what you see, but by what you know about God's truth. You aren't alone if you have to keep reminding yourself that God is with you. In the Bible, Joshua had to meditate day and night to maintain the presence of God in his life. When you feel vulnerable and alone, do you find it is harder or easier to let yourself be enveloped in God's powerful presence and steady strength?

Is it difficult to fathom His complete and utter desire to love you through every moment of your life?

_____

_____

_____

_____

_____

_____

_____

_____

_____

_____

_____

_____

ASK HIM

...to keep you from meddling in the problems He's handling for you today.

Okay, so you're a "take charge" kind of person. When you have a problem, all you really need is a little time to think it through, weigh your options, and figure out a solution.

Or maybe you're the kind of person who isn't as confident in your decisions but knows exactly the person you'd call for help when you need to solve a problem.

Either way, God wants to save you a heap of trouble by reminding you that He has everything under control. That means He needs you to stop trying to handle things that aren't yours to handle.

And yes, I do realize that you only interfere when you think He's not handling situations appropriately, but scripture says, "The Lord will fight for you; you need only to be still." It doesn't say, exhaust all other possibilities and then ask God for help.

He says, "Be still and know that I am God."

So, how about stepping aside and letting Him do His thing.

EXODUS 14:14

"The Lord will fight for you; you need only to be still."
(NIV)

PSALM 46:10

He says, "Be still, and know that I am God; I will be exalted
among the nations, I will be exalted in the earth." (NIV)

Journal

What problems do you continue to interfere with that God might be desperately trying to handle for you?

What's it going to take for you to step aside and let God be God?

_____

_____

_____

_____

_____

_____

_____

_____

_____

_____

_____

_____

_____

_____

Exodus 14:14 says, *"The Lord will fight for you; you need only to be still."*

How hard is it for you to be still and patient and wait on God to do His thing?

_____

_____

_____

_____

_____

_____

_____

_____

_____

_____

_____

_____

_____

_____

_____

_____

_____

ASK HIM

...to protect you from that twinge of resentment that creeps in when you see people being reckless and irresponsible with their health.

When you're passionately fighting for your life and you see other people being reckless and irresponsible with theirs, that twinge of resentment sure does feel justified.

There is even scripture that reads, *"But as for me, my feet had almost slipped; I had nearly lost my foothold. They have no struggles; their bodies are healthy and strong. They are free from the burdens common to man; they are not plagued by human ills"* (Ps. 73:2,4-5).

When we read this, it is comforting to know that these innate human feelings of resentment and envy not only existed centuries ago but also caused anguish and momentarily distracted them from who they were and how they wanted to live their lives.

We aren't any different today. No matter how noble our intentions, our humanness often creeps in and distracts us from being all we can possibly be with the circumstances we've been given.

PROVERBS 19:11

A person's wisdom yields patience; it is to one's glory to overlook an offense. (NIV)

HEBREWS 12:14-15

Make every effort to live in peace with everyone and to be holy; without holiness no one will see the Lord. See to it that no one falls short of the grace of God and that no bitter root grows up to cause trouble and defile many. (NIV)

Journal

Nothing screams resentment like passionately fighting for your life and seeing other people being reckless and irresponsible with theirs.

What has *their* behavior taught you about yourself?

_____

_____

_____

_____

_____

_____

_____

_____

_____

_____

_____

_____

_____

_____

B.C. (before cancer), were you ever reckless and irresponsible with your life?

Write a prayer sincerely asking God for His blessing and protection over people who are being reckless and irresponsible. Then thank Him for all the times He swooped in and saved you, especially when you were acting like a wild person.

_____

_____

_____

_____

_____

_____

_____

_____

_____

_____

_____

_____

_____

ASK HIM

…for the ability to thank that part of cancer that stopped your life and forced you to refocus your attention on all the things you already knew were most important.

Cancer makes things different. Your perspective is different. As much as we might hate to admit it, cancer can bring unexpected gifts for which we can be thankful.

There is something phenomenal and remarkable that occurs in the design of the human person when faced with life and death situations. When you're faced with your own mortality, your soul will propel its way into a more prominent place in your conscious thought.

When your soul is engaged, thoughts have new meaning…new value. Life has new meaning…new value. You judge less and appreciate more. You love more and fret less. You're less sensitive and more forgiving. You are more aware, more patient. Suddenly each small pleasure becomes more precious.

You don't ever have to be grateful for cancer! But you can be grateful for the ability to rethink things with an enhanced perspective of what is most important.

MATTHEW 6:33

But seek first his kingdom and his righteousness, and all these things will be given to you as well. (NIV)

ROMANS 12:2

Do not conform to the pattern of this world, but be transformed by the renewing of your mind. Then you will be able to test and approve what God's will is—his good, pleasing and perfect will. (NIV)

Journal

List a few things you find yourself concentrating on, things that you knew were important but you may have taken for granted before cancer. Then, list a few things that used to seem *so* important but now you couldn't care less about.

_____

_____

_____

_____

_____

_____

_____

_____

_____

_____

_____

_____

_____

Draw a line down the center of this page.

Make a comprehensive list of the good ways and the bad ways your cancer has changed you?

Why do you think cancer is responsible for those changes?

_____

_____

_____

_____

_____

_____

_____

_____

_____

_____

_____

_____

_____

_____

_____

ASK HIM

...for His continuous grace to help you push through the inconveniences cancer has forced on you and those you love.

Are you feeling inundated by all the changes cancer is forcing on you and your family? Constant changes. Constant adjustments. It's unnerving! It's annoying! It's frustrating! You know what else it is—it's typical and very normal. Most of us just don't like change. But it's important to feel and acknowledge the uneasiness and frustration of change.

Your circumstances don't change God; He remains the same. He wants to be your balance when all these changes start throwing you off center.

When you are anchored in the stability of God, that's where you'll find His grace. Grace is an unexplained feeling that doesn't let irritation and negativity, regardless of your circumstances, come in and affect your overall outlook. God never denies us His grace. He offers it new every day. So when the changes are making you feel rebellious, impatient, and exasperated, *Ask Him* for His abundant grace to push you through. By His grace you are able!

LAMENTATIONS 3:22-23

It is because of the Lord's mercy and lovingkindness that we are not consumed, because His [tender] compassions fail not. They are new every morning; great and abundant is Your stability and faithfulness. (AMP)

HEBREWS 13:8

Jesus Christ is the same yesterday, today, and forever. (ERV)

Journal

Sometimes changes shake things up, and all of a sudden something unexpectedly good ends up coming out of all the craziness. Has anything like that happened for you? What happened? What are the biggest adjustments, changes, and inconveniences you've had to deal with since you got your cancer diagnosis?

_____

_____

_____

_____

_____

_____

_____

_____

_____

_____

_____

_____

_____

You can't count on anything to stay the same anymore. The only thing that doesn't change is God. "The steadfast love of the Lord never ceases, His mercies never come to an end, they are new every morning…" (Lamentations 3:22).

Let Him be your calm in the storm when the inconveniences of cancer feel like they are relentlessly crashing over you. What graces do you need "stat" from God right this minute?

_____

_____

_____

_____

_____

_____

_____

_____

_____

_____

_____

_____

ASK HIM

...to heap "ginormous" blessings on all the caregivers whose tireless efforts, genuine goodness, and selfless compassion make this world a better place because they're here.

No one will ever know the indescribable gift it is to have dependable people in your life when you are in crisis. What is most amazing about caregivers is that they eagerly take it upon themselves to step in to help. Unless you have been in the humbling position to need help, you cannot imagine how grateful and relieved you feel to have people who'll go out of their way to make your life easier.

It is God's divine compassion manifested in human beings—*some who are total strangers!* To experience this level of unselfishness and generosity by other people is life changing.

It's emotional just to think about. And even though you may think there is nothing you can do to reciprocate at this time, there absolutely is! You can pray for God's favor to rest on every person who has tirelessly and unselfishly been available to help you and those closest to you to persevere.

1 THESSALONIANS 5:12-13

Now brothers and sisters, we ask you to recognize the value of those who work hard among you—those who, as followers of the Lord, care for you and tell you how to live. Show them the highest respect and love because of the work they do. (ERV)

PSALM 41:1-3

Those who help the poor succeed will get many blessings. When trouble comes, the Lord will save them. The Lord will protect them and save their lives. He will bless them in this land. He will not let their enemies harm them. When they are sick in bed, the Lord will give them strength and make them well! (ERV)

Journal

In your journal, take time today to jot down a little note or prayer of gratitude for the caregivers who are making such a huge difference in your life.

_____

_____

_____

_____

_____

_____

_____

_____

_____

_____

_____

_____

_____

_____

_____

_____

What or who has surprised you the most in your greatest time of need?

_____

_____

_____

_____

_____

_____

_____

_____

_____

_____

_____

_____

_____

_____

_____

_____

_____

ASK HIM

...to help you remember that there are times when unanswered prayer is the best possible outcome.

What are you fervently praying for? When it comes to our prayers, we may *think* we know what's best, but the truth is that we don't have a clue.

We would probably be shocked to know how many times our unanswered prayers actually end up being monumental blessings in disguise.

What we need to remember is that God's best is far beyond our best. And truth be told, if we got what we prayed for all the time, we'd probably be a complete mess.

My friend and author Matthew Kelly says it perfectly. "God wants your future to be bigger than your past."

So when you find yourself praying...and praying...and praying, and nothing happens, it isn't because He doesn't care about the things you want. It's because He wants something more, something better.

When you make your requests and prayers known to God, try prefacing them with sincerely wanting His most excellent outcome, in every area of your life.

ISAIAH 55:8-9

"For my thoughts are not your thoughts, neither are your ways my ways," declares the Lord. "As the heavens are higher than the earth, so are my ways higher than your ways and my thoughts than your thoughts." (NIV)

1 JOHN 5:14

We can come to God with no doubts. This means that when we ask God for things (and those things agree with what God wants for us), God cares about what we say. (ERV)

Journal

What are you fervently praying for? Don't be shy. Make a list. Be specific.

_____

_____

_____

_____

_____

_____

_____

_____

_____

_____

_____

_____

_____

_____

_____

_____

_____

_____

_____

Write out your prayer requests today, but preface them with: "Lord, what I most sincerely desire is Your best possible outcome, in every area of my life."

Does this prayer request change your perspective on what you've been praying for and how you've been asking?

_____

_____

_____

_____

_____

_____

_____

_____

_____

_____

_____

_____

_____

_____

_____

ASK HIM

…to help you regard the time between your last day of treatment and the follow up appointment *not* as a waiting period for the cancer to return, but a period to emerge inspired, with a renewed sense of purpose.

Talk about altering your day-to-day existence! One moment you're in the ordinary everyday "living your life" mode and the next you're in a "saving your life" mode!

Instead of going for coffee, you're going for a scan. Instead of spending time with friends, you're spending time in treatment. Then one day you finish treatment and the doctor says; "See you in three months!" And voila, everything goes right back to normal. Not!

He wants you to be *grateful*, acknowledging your new sense of self, and grateful for the challenges you've overcome that laid the foundation for this newer, stronger you.

He wants you *inspired* to give back in honor of those who've helped you grow to be the person you are today.

He wants you *believing* that He is weaving a perfect plan for your life *even* through this cancer experience.

God sees this time as a perfect time to watch you soar…renewed, inspired, and encouraged.

2 CORINTHIANS 3:16-18

But when someone changes and follows the Lord, that covering is taken away. The Lord is the Spirit, and where the Spirit of the Lord is, there is freedom. And our faces are not covered. We all show the Lord's glory, and we are being changed to be like him. This change in us brings more and more glory, which comes from the Lord, who is the Spirit. (ERV)

COLOSSIANS 1:9-12

Since the day we heard these things about you, we have continued praying for you. This is what we pray: that God will make you completely sure of what he wants by giving you all the wisdom and spiritual understanding you need; that this will help you live in a way that brings honor to the Lord and pleases him in every way; that your life will produce good works of every kind and that you will grow in your knowledge of God; that God will strengthen you with his own great power, so that you will be patient and not give up when troubles come. Then you will be happy and give thanks to the Father. He has made you able to have what he has promised to give all his holy people, who live in the light. (ERV)

Journal

What renewed sense of purpose do you think God is calling you to?

What can you take from your cancer experience that will be the greatest value to you as you move forward in life?

_____

_____

_____

_____

_____

_____

_____

_____

_____

_____

_____

_____

_____

_____

_____

The truth is, it's tricky to shift yourself out of cancer gear. It takes some adjusting and transitioning to re-acclimate yourself into your daily life again.

There is no such thing as "back to normal." What there is however, is a new normal and a new you.

Write down some of the things that are hindering your ability to transition back into your daily life again. Be specific.

_____

_____

_____

_____

_____

_____

_____

_____

_____

_____

_____

_____

_____

_____

ASK HIM

...to help you find the balance between conscientiously listening to your body and completely obsessing over it.

With cancer, you become acutely aware of everything your body does and feels. Every ache, every pain, every sensation causes you alarm. You don't want to be neurotic, but you don't want to be foolish either. So you obsess about what might be going on inside your body.

Keeping your body on this type of high alert status keeps you mentally stressed. God wants to give you the grace to subdue and tame this stress. He promises that He will keep in perfect peace those whose minds are steadfast in their trust for Him.

So with *your* trust and *His* grace, you will find the balance to be conscientiously attuned to the changes in your body while resisting the impulse to completely obsess about them.

God doesn't want you to be full of confusion and torment. Scripture says that the Spirit God gave us does not make us afraid. His Spirit is a source of power and love and self-control. Let that spirit abide in you today!

PSALM 16:8-9

I keep my eyes always on the Lord. With him at my right hand, I will not be shaken. Therefore my heart is glad and my tongue rejoices; my body also will rest secure. (NIV)

LAMENTATIONS 3:22-23

It is because of the Lord's mercy and loving-kindness that we are not consumed, because His [tender] compassions fail not. They are new every morning; great and abundant is Your stability and faithfulness. (AMP)

Journal

Obsessing over every ache, pain, and sensation in your body keeps it on high alert, which exhausts the body and deprives it of the vital rest it needs to heal.

Get with your doctor and make a plan about what's normal and to be expected, and what's not. This will allow you to be cautious, not careless, about the changes in your body.

Write the plan on this page.

_____

_____

_____

_____

_____

_____

_____

_____

_____

_____

_____

There is a way for you to direct your thoughts and guide your imagination toward a relaxed and spiritual state. You start by imagining all the details of a safe, comfortable place like a meadow, sitting under a huge shade tree or on a beautiful beach with crystal blue water. In your journal, describe your "special place" and include as many details as you can.

When you are obsessing about life, ask God to go with you to your special place where your body will rest secure; you will walk in perfect peace and find the serenity you need for healing.

_____

_____

_____

_____

_____

_____

_____

_____

_____

_____

ASK HIM

...for the strength to believe that His commitment *never* waivers. He will *never* leave you. He will *never* fail you. He will *never* forsake you.

Do you feel sometimes like God has forgotten about you? That maybe He has lost interest in you and moved on to someone else?

It says in the Bible, *"Be strong and courageous for the Lord your God goes with you; He will never leave you nor forsake you. No one will be able to stand against you all the days of your life. As I was with Moses, so I will be with you; I will never leave you nor forsake you."*

This is God's unwavering commitment to you. This is His absolute truth to you. When you love God, He delivers you and sets you on high. He even gave His angels special charge over you to accompany, defend, and preserve you in all your ways. He never gives up on you.

He will never abandon you. Believe that God's love and Christ's perseverance will fortify and direct your every step.

He has been intimately involved in every facet of your life since before you were born. He is unfaltering. He is unwavering. He is unrelenting. *He will...never...leave...you!*

DEUTERONOMY 31:6

"Be strong and courageous. Do not be afraid or terrified because of them, for the Lord your God goes with you; he will never leave you nor forsake you." (NIV)

JOSHUA 1:5

No one will be able to stand against you all the days of your life. As I was with Moses, so I will be with you; I will never leave you nor forsake you. (NIV)

Journal

This is God's unwavering commitment to you. This is His absolute truth to you. Be strengthened, be encouraged, be confident. *He will...never...leave...you!*

Those are powerful words. How does it make you feel to have this unwavering commitment from God?

Does it bring you a sense of consoling relief? Why?

_____

_____

_____

_____

_____

_____

_____

_____

_____

_____

_____

_____

_____

Your God will always be *for* you, never against you. He will always be the place from which your help comes.

How will you stay steadfast and determined to live by and trust that truth every day?

Write a short prayer you can repeat to yourself whenever you begin to feel even the tiniest bit abandoned.

_____

_____

_____

_____

_____

_____

_____

_____

_____

_____

_____

_____

_____

_____

ASK HIM
...just ASK HIM!